WOMEN'S SOCCER

A Guide to Coaching and Training

JANE HASLAM

THE CROWOOD PRESS

First published in 2010 by
The Crowood Press Ltd
Ramsbury, Marlborough
Wiltshire SN8 2HR

www.crowood.com

© Jane Haslam 2010

British Library Cataloguing-in-Publication Data
A catalogue record for this book is available from the British Library.

ISBN 978 1 84797 221 7

Disclaimer
The author and the publisher do not accept any responsibility in any manner whatsoever for any
error or omission, or any loss, damage, injury, adverse outcome, or liability of any kind incurred as
a result of the use of any of the information contained in this book, or reliance upon it. Since the
physical activities in this book may be too strenuous in nature for some readers to engage in safely,
it is essential that a doctor be consulted before undertaking training.

Illustration credits
All images are © Jane Haslam (www.janehaslamphotography.com), except the following: pages 8,
134, 138 and 143, © Nikki Ebbage; and page 14, © Mark Hodsman.

Typeset by Bookcraft Ltd, Stroud, Gloucestershire
Printed and bound in Malaysia by Times Offset (M) Sdn Bhd

CONTENTS

DEDICATION

For my Mum and Dad

Football was my way of life from a very early age and I am so lucky that my parents finally gave up on their aspirations for their little girl and threw themselves wholeheartedly behind my passion. I know I've made them very proud.

ACKNOWLEDGEMENTS

This book is the culmination of my own personal journey through the game, so to all those individuals who I have met, or played against, or coached, or coached with, or watched, or listened to, my heartfelt thanks for all that I have learnt.

Many thanks and best wishes to all at Linby Girls and Ladies FC who gave up their time to help me with the illustrations for this book.

I am especially grateful to Nikki, Nitin and David. Without your encouragement and belief in me I would have never finished these words.

Jane has an extensive background in football and a large amount of relevant experience in the field of player development. Her book addresses many of the issues specific to the women's game and I'm sure you'll find her insights a valuable addition to your library.

Hope Powell, England Women's National Coach

LEFT: *Claire Rafferty of England shields the ball from Danielle Foxhoven of the USA.*

CHAPTER I

A BRIEF HISTORY OF WOMEN'S FOOTBALL IN BRITAIN

During the first ten years of the twenty-first century, women's football has truly become a global phenomenon, driving and providing sporting opportunities for girls and women all over the world. It is played by over 26 million players in approximately 150 countries and according to statistics released by FIFA, football's international governing body, the game is still growing at an accelerating rate.

In many countries, the structure for girls and women to compete is as well-developed as that in the male game and international competition is comprehensive. FIFA organizes World Cup tournaments for Senior, Under-20 and Under-17 players, as well as the Olympic tournament. Feeding into this, each of the six continental confederations organizes its own official championships. In Europe, for example, UEFA organizes championships at Senior, Under-19 and Under-17 levels involving over forty nations. On a national level, many of the more advanced women's football nations have a pyramid of playing and developmental opportunities, as well as professional or semi-professional teams competing in national leagues. More than ever before women can aspire to pursue high-profile and successful football careers in both the men's and the women's game.

The history of women's football can be traced back to the origins of Association Football in late-Victorian England and is a fascinating story in its own right. For the many women involved, the story is characterized by their constant struggle merely to win acceptance and respectability in what is essentially still a male-dominated sport. That women's football has reached this point at all is testament to their collective determination in the face of prejudice. Now the fight for acceptance has moved to new parts of the world. Today's pioneers in African and Muslim nations have history on their side, as well as a wealth of role models, from which they can gain strength, inspiration and respectability.

A FINE ALL-ROUND PLAYER.

LEFT: Argentina making preparations to play against the USA.

Typical postcard humour illustrating the attitudes of the day.

Pioneers

The first few minutes were sufficient to show that football by women, if the British Ladies be taken as a criterion, is totally out of the question. A footballer requires speed, judgement, skill, and pluck. Not one of these four qualities was apparent on Saturday. For the most part, the ladies wandered aimlessly over the field at an ungraceful jog-trot.

Report from the *Daily Sketch* in March 1895, following the first recorded women's football match at Crouch End, North London

The modern game of men's football can trace its origins to Victorian Britain of the mid-nineteenth century, where it flourished among the working classes in the great industrial cities. Its simplicity meant that, by the end of the century, the game had spread into Europe and, via the British Empire, to all corners of the globe. Professionalism was formally accepted in 1885 and the first Football League was formed in 1888. For women, this became their first major exposure to the game as the league's administrators were becoming preoccupied with the poor behaviour of male supporters at football matches. A suggestion was made that their behaviour would improve if they were accompanied to matches and so an initiative to allow free entry to women was created. It is thought that over 2,000 women attended a Preston North End match in April 1885, after which the idea survived for over 10 years and then was only discontinued because it became too popular.

It comes as no surprise that, having watched the game, women wanted to play it. Research would suggest that the delightfully named Nettie Honeyball was the very first pioneer of the women's game. In 1894 she placed an advertisement in a North London newspaper that resulted in the formation of the British Ladies Football Club. Eventually the ladies trained twice a week under the guidance of Tottenham Hotspur professional JW Julian and played their first official match at Crouch End in North London on 23 March 1895. For this game, the club organized its players into two teams to represent North and South London. For the record, the North, playing in red, beat the South, playing in blue, by a score-line of 7–1.

The British Ladies went on to play more exhibition games at grounds throughout England and Scotland in front of interested crowds. Attendances numbered from just a few hundred up into the thousands, with the largest recorded as 8,000 for a match played at St James' Park in Newcastle. Although there were some positive comments, the media of the day were generally scathing, thereby voicing the prejudice that women footballers would have to face for much of the next 100 years.

The Rise and Fall of Women's Football in Early Twentieth-Century Britain

The Council feels impelled to express the strong opinion that the game is quite unsuitable for females and ought not to be encouraged.

The FA Council (England), 1921

British society during the early years of the twentieth century was beginning to see small but significant changes in the everyday lives of women. The growth of the suffragette movement was one good reason for this and another was the impact of the Great War fought from 1914 to 1918. Indeed it was the war that really accelerated these seeds of social change. With men increasingly conscripted to the battlefields of Europe, women had to take a more pivotal role in the workforce, so that by the end of hostilities in 1918, nearly five million women were working in jobs formerly carried out by men.

In a society that was starved of entertainment and suffering greatly from the 'war to end all wars', it is little wonder that these new workers began to seek diversions and turned to football during their break time. In fact it is recorded that the Prime Minister, David Lloyd George, actually encouraged women to play, as he saw their involvement as a positive force for morale, as well as an excellent way to raise funds for the war effort.

By 1916, factories all over Britain were organizing matches between women's sides, with all the monies raised being given to various war charities. Women's football was becoming, in the process, inextricably linked with fund-raising efforts on the home front. In a very short space of time these games became very popular and one such match, played on Christmas Day 1917 at Deepdale, the home of Preston North End, had an attendance of over 10,000 people. It raised £200 for war charities (equivalent to £41,000 today) and was the first game of any kind that had been played on the pitch since the suspension of the Football League at the outbreak of the war, three years earlier.

It was during this era that the Dick, Kerr's Ladies Football Team was founded and their exploits provide an intriguing historical sub-plot to the growth of women's football in Great Britain during the first half of the twentieth century. The team was from an engineering factory located in Preston, Lancashire – a county that already had a strong football tradition. Five of the original twelve men's Football League clubs hailed from Lancashire, therefore it should come as no surprise that Preston was to become the epicentre of a golden age for women's football. From their formation the Dick,

Dick, Kerr's Ladies Football Team pictured in 1921.

Kerr's Ladies Football Team was managed by Alfred Frankland, who was an office worker with the company. His association with them lasted for thirty-eight years, right up until 1955 when ill health forced him to retire. In fact he was so dedicated to his team that in 1923 he resigned from his job at the factory because the new owners attempted to curtail his football activities.

The Dick, Kerr's Ladies played regular charity games all over Britain and, once the war ended, continued their charity matches in order to raise money for the wounded and the needy. As their fame spread across Britain, the best players in the country travelled to Preston to join the team. They were given jobs at the factory and paid a ten shillings match fee plus travel expenses, though it should be noted that the fees were relatively small in relation to the sums raised for charity. For example, in September 1919, a match played at St James' Park against Newcastle United raised £1,200 for local war charities (in modern terms approximately £250,000) in front of a gate of 35,000 people.

By 1920, the women's game was well-established and crowds were consistently large, in some cases attendances even exceeded those at the newly restarted Football League fixtures. A period of four weeks over the Christmas and New Year period in 1920–21 saw three remarkable games with a cumulative attendance of 100,000 spectators and nearly £6,000 raised for the Unemployed Ex-Servicemen's Distress Fund. The first on 16 December was played at Deepdale in front of

12,000 spectators and it ended in a 4–0 win for the Dick, Kerr's Ladies against a representative team from the rest of England. It was filmed for Pathé News and was the first ever women's floodlit match, utilizing two anti-aircraft searchlights, over forty carbide flares, as well as a number of whitewashed footballs. Ten days later, 53,000 attended a fixture at Goodison Park, the home of Everton FC, and this is still the largest recorded attendance for a women's fixture in Great Britain. The final game of the series was held at Old Trafford in Manchester, where a crowd of 35,000 attended.

In 1920, Dick, Kerr's Ladies competed in the first recorded women's international fixture, a series of eight games played in spring and autumn against France. For the record, they won five of the eight games, drew two and lost one. The quality of play was highly praised at the time, although one player stood head and shoulders above the rest. Lily Parr was a teenage sensation who joined the team from St Helens in 1919. She played for them throughout the rest of her career, playing her last game in August 1950 at the age of 45. She died of cancer in 1978 and in 1992 was inducted into the National Football Museum hall of fame. The local Preston newspaper wrote of her in 1920:

There is probably no greater football prodigy in the whole country. Not only has she speed and excellent ball control, but her admirable physique enables her to brush off challenges from defenders who tackle her. She amazes

Women's team from the Greenwood & Batley munitions factory in Leeds, Yorkshire.

the crowd where ever she goes by the way she swings the ball clean across the goalmouth to the opposite wing.

Following the end of the First World War, it is clear to see that women's football was flourishing in Britain, but unfortunately the halcyon days were almost over, and sadly there was to be no further development. Soldiers returning from the battlegrounds of Europe had no concept of the changes that had taken place in society. Their attitudes were unchanged from those they had harboured pre-war; in fact they had been hardened by the horrors that they had witnessed. Many found it difficult to accept that their wives, girlfriends and sisters were wearing shorts and playing what they saw as a man's game. The other problem was that women's fixtures had become totally bound up with fund-raising for war charities, but as time passed the need for this type of fund-raising was slowly ebbing away.

Looking back, it is clear that to sustain itself the game needed to establish a regular fixture list. This never happened and, as war charities began to disappear, the women began to play for causes that were far more controversial. When matches were staged in aid of the miners in the North of England, women's football was seen to be creating a link to the Labour movement

Doris. A player with the Henley Girls Football Team 1920.

MILESTONES IN THE DEVELOPMENT OF WOMEN'S FOOTBALL

Date	Event
1895	First recorded women's game. Played at Crouch End North London.
1920	53,000 attend a match at Goodison Park, the home of Everton FC.
1921	The FA bans women's football in England.
1922	The Canadian FA decrees that football is an unsuitable sport for women.
1932	Italy and France establish women's leagues.
1955	The Dutch Women's Football Federation is formed.
1968	Italian Women's Football Federation is formed.
1969	English Women's Football Association formed including teams in Scotland and Ireland.
1970	The DFB rescind their ban and formally recognise women's football in West Germany.
1971	West Germany has over 1,000 affiliated women's teams. The KNVB formally take over the administration of women's football in the Netherlands. The English FA lifts the ban on women players.
1972	The Scottish Women's FA is formed. Title IX legislation in the USA provides a mandate for gender equality in sport.
1973	The Danish FA organises an official women's league competition.
1976	The Norwegian FA introduces women's football.
1978	The Swedish FA takes over responsibility for running the women's game.
1981	Women's varsity soccer programme established in the USA.
1982	1.5 million female players in the USA.
1983	FIFA instructs its member associations to take a greater responsibility for women's football.
1984	The first European championship is won by Sweden.
1986	The Italian FA takes over the running of the women's game.
1988	The Greek FA recognises women's football.
1993	The Football Association takes full control of the women's game in England.
1999	The Women's World Cup hosted by the USA attracts record crowds. 90,185 attend the final.
2001	Inaugural season of the American Women's Professional League. First European Club Championship won by FFC Frankfurt.
2009	Women's professional soccer in the USA resumes.

and, by association, now playing a dangerous political game. This was unacceptable to the middle classes, the establishment and those charged with administering the game at the Football Association. Action was swift and merciless. At an FA Council meeting on 5 December 1921 a resolution was passed that outlawed the game. Overnight women were banned from using FA affiliated pitches and anyone who was found to be assisting women's teams would be banned for life from membership of the Football Association. The game was out in the cold and its decline was inevitable.

Playing On in Barren Times

Women's football brings the game into disrepute.
Kent County FA (1947)

In 1921 when the FA outlawed the game, there were 150 teams in England and, as the news sunk in, many resolved to fight the ban. Alfred Frankland, the Dick, Kerr's Team Manager declared:

The team will continue to play, if the organisers of charity matches will provide grounds, even if we have to play on ploughed fields.

For a brief time the clubs were united; within five days they had organized a meeting that led to the formation of the English Ladies FA. At last women's football had a voice and structure. In their first full season, the ELFA established a national Women's Cup competition, which Stoke Ladies eventually won, as well as tabling some interesting ideas to adapt the game for women. There was a suggestion of smaller pitches and lighter balls,

though it is difficult to see how these could have been implemented by a game fighting for recognition and teetering on the edge of extinction. Ultimately though the FA ban had a far-reaching effect and, despite a bright start, the ELFA ended in failure. In reality there were never enough teams to establish meaningful competition, nor a stable league structure. In time it was inevitable that interest would wane, as it became increasingly difficult to find games, facilities and personnel.

The exception to this was Dick, Kerr's who continued to play charity games and unofficial internationals. In 1922 they embarked on a tour of Canada, although, upon arriving in the country, found that the Canadian FA had also banned women from playing the game. Undaunted they changed their itinerary and headed into the United States where they played seven games against men's teams from the fledgling American Soccer League. It is testament to the quality of their play that they won three of their games, drew two and lost only two. In 1923, the French ladies returned to England again to play a series of matches against the Dick, Kerr's team, one of which took place on the rugby pitch at Cardiff Arms Park in Wales.

The time between the wars passed and the FA ban strangled the life out of women's football, matches taking place with ever-decreasing frequency. It also became clear that pressure was being applied by the FA to ensure that the ban wasn't breached. When English Electric took over the Dick, Kerr's factory in 1923, the new management ended all association with the team, withdrawing funding and facilities. However, Alfred Frankland and his team were made of sterner stuff; they renamed themselves Preston Ladies and continued to play matches. In 1937 their claim to be World Champions was challenged by Edinburgh Ladies, the Champions

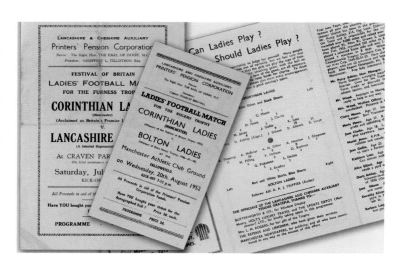

A selection of Corinthian Ladies programmes from the 1952–53 season.

Arsenal Ladies FC, England's most successful women's football team, celebrate winning the FA Cup in 2009.

of Scotland. The game took place on 8 September 1937 amid a frenzy of publicity reminiscent of the 20 years previously. The match was won easily by the Preston girls. Lily Parr scored one and 15-year-old newcomer, Joan Whalley, scored another. Afterwards the team was feted at a World Championship Victory Dinner in Preston.

Recreation throughout Britain all but ceased during the Second World War. Due to rationing and harsher conditions on the Home Front, there was to be no repeat of the glory years of women's football during this war.

In the immediate post-war period, women did resume their matches but there was to be no weakening of attitudes at the FA and they just as vigorously applied their ban on the game. In 1947, the Kent County Football Association suspended a referee because he was working as a manager and trainer with Kent Ladies Football Club.

1949 saw the formation of a new team, the Corinthians Ladies; they were from Manchester and were destined to follow in the footsteps of the Dick, Kerr's Ladies, playing only for charitable causes, on cricket pitches, rugby grounds and even greyhound tracks

throughout Britain. By the summer of 1953 they had played over 100 games and raised £14,000 for charity. They also ran a reserve side called the Nomads and often, because of a lack of local opposition, the match would be played between the Corinthians and Nomads. Towards the end of the decade, Corinthians became globetrotters, organizing fixtures abroad via the Red Cross. In 1957 and 1958 they toured Germany twice, as well as Portugal and Madeira. In 1959 it was a trip to Holland followed up by South America and Ireland in 1960. 1961 saw them playing in Italy and then their last tour was in 1966 to North Africa. Overall, in the space of seventeen years they played 287 games worldwide, winning 256 and raising over £70,000 for charity.

The Modern Game

The future of football is feminine.
Sepp Blatter, President of FIFA

The game that we have in place today, although it has its roots in the early twentieth century, it is very different from anything that could have been envisaged even back in the golden age. Development began to gather momentum throughout Europe during the 1960s and 70s when the foundations of many of today's playing structures were put in place.

In Britain, an English victory in the 1966 men's World Cup stimulated an interest in football to hitherto unprecedented levels. As spectator numbers rose and participation boomed, women began to play in increasing numbers once again. This time a structure to administer the game was high on the agenda, the Women's Football Association was founded in 1969 and it very quickly established a platform for discussion with the FA, as well as representation for English, Scottish and Irish

teams. In May 1971, the WFA Mitre Cup was launched after sponsorship from the Yorkshire-based sportswear manufacturer was obtained. Then, in 1972, the first official international game was played at Greenock in Scotland when England beat the Scots 3–2 in a closely fought game.

In continental Europe the pace was even faster. Italy, through sponsorship, had established a formal semi-professional league for women; then, in 1970 and 1971, two unofficial world cups were organized in Italy and Mexico. UEFA, the sport's European governing body, had monitored the growth of the game carefully and at a meeting in 1971, recommended that each member association

MILESTONES IN THE DEVELOPMENT OF INTERNATIONAL WOMEN'S FOOTBALL

Date	Event
1956	West Germany play the Netherlands in a first official international fixture.
1972	The first official international takes place on British soil. England play Scotland in Greenock.
1973	Sweden and Finland play their first official international match.
1974	The Scandinavian federations organise the first Nordic Cup competition.
1975	New Zealand and Thailand play in the first final of the Asian Confederation cup.
1985	The USA play their first official international match in Italy.
1986	A Chinese National team tours Europe. Canada plays its first international match against the USA. First Under-16 International between Sweden and Norway.
1988	Brazil play their first international match against Spain. Swede Gunilla Paijkull becomes the first female coach of a national team.
1990	Sweden and Germany introduce Under-19 International teams.
1991	Brazilian woman Claudia de Vasconcelos Guedes becomes the first woman to referee a match in a FIFA World Cup Competition. The USA win the first FIFA Women's World Cup.
1992	The USA introduce Under-16 and Under-20 National teams.
1994	The Republic of Ireland introduce Under-16 and Under-20 National teams.
1996	The First Olympic tournament is won by the USA in front of 76,489 spectators. Tina Theune Mayer becomes the German National Coach. Marika Domanski Lyfors becomes the Swedish National Coach.
1997	England introduce an Under-19 National team.
1998	First UEFA Under-19 Championship is won by Denmark. Hope Powell is appointed English National Team Coach.
2002	The first FIFA Under-19 World Cup is held in Canada and won by the USA.
2008	The first FIFA Under-17 World Cup is held in New Zealand, and won by Korea DPR

take control of the women's game in their country. Some nations embraced this directive very quickly, establishing themselves at the forefront of the women's game for the next thirty years. Sweden, Norway, Denmark and Germany developed structures for players, coaches and administrators, so that, when FIFA introduced the first Women's World Cup Competition in 1991, they were ready to compete on a world stage.

It was only in 1993 that the English FA followed suit, beginning a slow but steady development that has allowed them to emulate their Northern European neighbours. The FA implemented a comprehensive nationwide football development plan that embraced and encompassed all levels of the girls' and women's game. The same is true in Wales, Ireland and Scotland, with opportunities for girls to play being greater than ever before. In many schools, football is on the curriculum, there is a thriving league structure and clubs are able to cater for players of all age groups and levels of experience. The FA has also established a comprehensive pathway for players to progress to elite levels. In 1998, Hope Powell was appointed England Women's national team coach and, under her leadership, the international programme is beginning to achieve success on the world stage. The structure has developed a new generation of female players and coaches who are capable of competing at the highest levels of the game. In the twelve months from October 2008 to September 2009, England Women's squads collectively achieved their best-ever results, with the Under-17s finishing fourth at the inaugural world championship in New Zealand, the Under-20s reaching the quarter-finals of the world championships in Chile, the Senior women losing to Germany in the European Championship final, and the Under-19 squad becoming European Champions for the first time after beating Sweden 2–0 in the European Championship final.

Truly the indomitable spirit of those twentieth-century pioneers lives on in their modern counterparts and undoubtedly women's football is here to stay. Women's football has many fascinating stories to tell, its ambitions may be bigger and bolder than in the past, but undoubtedly the world has truly embraced the beautiful game.

- There is only the goalkeeper closer to the goal than her.
- Blue player B is offside.

In the real world, the decision for the referee is complicated at best. The presence of two teams muddies the picture, and with attacking players constantly seeking to gain the advantage over defenders, the judgements can be very fine. On the television, an instant action replay provides a second chance for the spectator to make up their mind. Unfortunately the referee doesn't have that luxury; she has to make the decision in a split second, often from an area of the pitch where the view is limited.

Foul Play

The laws are very clear in relation to foul play or misconduct, and there is little room for interpretation by the referee or her assistants. Serious foul play will result in a direct free kick or penalty against the team

Arsenal's Suzanne Grant takes a tumble against Sunderland.

committing the offence, which means that a goal can be scored directly from the kick.

Serious offences would include violence or attempted violence towards an opponent. The list of actions is as follows:

- Tripping.
- Jumping.
- Pushing.
- Charging.
- Kicking.
- Striking.
- Spitting.
- Holding.

Note: Deliberate handball by an outfield player is also punished as a serious offence.

Less serious infringements are punished by indirect free kicks and the list of offences includes impeding a player, time-wasting and unsporting conduct. The award of an indirect free kick means that another player has to touch the ball before a goal can be scored.

Referees generally try to use a common-sense approach to control the game and keep it flowing. However, if it becomes overheated, there are sterner sanctions available. A red and yellow card system is used to denote official punishment, where yellow is a warning and red an immediate expulsion from the field of play. Players who receive a card during a game will then be punished according to the severity of the offence; this could mean a fine or even a ban from playing for a specified period of time.

Modifications

So far this chapter has outlined the official rules for the game of football, a game for adult players, on large pitches, with two teams of eleven players. However, these are completely inappropriate for teams of young players or even novice adults. For such competitions, the rules can and should be modified in order to create an environment where the players can play and develop, but most of all have fun doing so.

Small-sided matches, where the laws of the game have been adapted, pitches have been scaled down and numbers of players within a team reduced, are already well-established within grassroots girls' and women's football, but it should still be emphasized that the advantages of using smaller teams and pitches far outweigh any disadvantages. The games are very fluid and fast moving, as well as being realistic; everyone is involved and, more often than not, playing with a smile on their face. Individual players have more touches on the ball and there are more chances in front of the goal.

Small-sided football matches provide a fun, safe environment, as well as making a massive contribution to the overall development of both individuals and teams – an important factor for the continued and sustained growth of the girls' and women's game.

A Brief Interview with Hope Powell OBE, England Women's National Team Coach

With more than a decade in charge of the women's international programme, Hope Powell has become an important force in the world of women's football. Her achievements both on a personal level and within football should serve as an inspiration to women and girls everywhere who dare to have a dream.

She began playing at the age of eleven for Millwall Lionesses back in 1978 and went on to have a distinguished career winning the FA Cup three times, as well as numerous domestic championships. She made her England debut at the age of sixteen, representing her country sixty-six times and culminating in an appearance at the Women's World Cup in Sweden in 1995.

She was appointed as the England Women's Head Coach in 1998 at the age of thirty-one and went on to become the first female to achieve the prestigious pro-coaching licence in 2003. Under her guidance the international player pathway has become a strong and well-respected programme, and the England women's team has risen steadily through the FIFA world rankings to become one of the top international teams in Europe.

In 2002 Hope was awarded the OBE in recognition of her services to sport.

Hope Powell.

Question: You have been national coach since 1998, what are your aims for the future?

Answer: A lot of hard work has gone into the development of all our squads and players since I was appointed to the job and I know that we are starting to reap the benefits of that work. Our secret has probably been consistency and continuity so with the senior side and the Under-19s both reaching the finals of the European championships in 2009 the future looks bright.

Question: When you select a player for the national team what are the most important attributes that you look for?

Answer: Well that's a difficult question to answer in a short sentence because there are so many variables as well as differences between age groups. We have an extensive scouting network and try to look at a player from every angle; we'll assess her ability and her current form, look at her attitude and her desire, then try to measure it against her potential for the future.

Question: In your opinion what attributes will the complete female player possess?

Answer: Well as I said, performance is defined by such a wide range of qualities that it is difficult to think that any one player could ever possess them all. She certainly needs to have talent on the pitch, be able to play at pace and have a strong character, but then there is so much more that goes into the mix.

Question: What advice would you give to a young player starting out in the game?

Answer: If you love playing, don't be put off by the demands and the hard work. It's a great game and, for the lucky few that make it, the rewards are worth it.

CHAPTER 3

THE COACH IN THE FEMALE GAME

Every group of people requires a leader, someone to provide motivation and direction, inspiration and purpose. For most women's football teams that person is the coach. It's a powerful position with influence over others, because the coach is generally the person responsible for all aspects in relation to the team's performance and results. They are always the one to blame when things go wrong, yet are often taken for granted when things go right.

Coaches come from a wide range of backgrounds; they may be professionals with years of experience in football or an enthusiastic parent who has volunteered in order to help the team out. Yet at whatever end of the spectrum they belong and at whatever level they work, the role of the coach is an undeniably complex one. It is always time-consuming and very hard work, but when things go right, it can be an incredibly rewarding experience.

This chapter provides a general outline of the qualities required to become a coach and stresses the importance of employing a consistent coaching philosophy. It then goes on to explore the dynamics found within female groups and teams, before finally making recommendations as to how a coach can shape an environment in which female players can flourish.

The Role of a Coach

The coach is responsible for team preparation. Through their expertise, the performance of the team is optimized and the potential of each player developed. Specific aspects of the role may change, depending upon the club and the level at which the coach is working, but in practice, coaching is as complex in grassroots football as it is in international football. As the diagram below illustrates the role can be broken down into three main headings, which require the coach to have a diverse range of skills and qualities:

- Leader. The coach provides direction, as well as inspiration and motivation.
- Educator. No matter how experienced the team, the coach is required to improve performance.

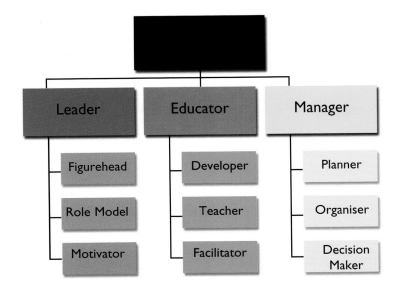

LEFT: *Creating rapport with a young player.*

RIGHT: *The varied roles of the coach.*

This entails being able to teach in a variety of styles, in order to get the message across to all players.

- Manager. Success in such a complex role requires structure. The coach must be able to think both long and short term, in order to provide consistent day-to-day management of the environment.

The Personal Qualities of a Coach

Working with any group of people is a constant challenge, where individuals are prone to put their needs and expectations above those of the group. In the female sporting environment, the complexity is heightened because confidence and mood can also be unpredictably fragile.

With this in mind, the coach will need a strong personality supported by a diverse range of personal attributes.

There are six key qualities that are prerequisites for success.

A male coach providing the pre-game motivation.

Enthusiasm

- Football is a game of extremes and emotions, which the coach has to cope with at all times. By maintaining an enthusiastic approach, the environment created will be consistent and generally positive.
- A positive approach affects the attitude of everyone associated with the team, building rapport and respect.
- Enthusiasm is also associated with perseverance and patience, which a coach needs in abundance when working to develop performance.

Knowledge

- A coach can never have too much knowledge, as knowledge brings about understanding and therefore increases the chances of success.
- It is specifically important that the coach has a good knowledge of the game, especially the women's game, as well as an understanding of how football is played both tactically and technically.
- The coach also needs a wider appreciation of other factors that contribute towards performance, such as how individuals learn and people management.

Communication

- Enthusiasm and knowledge are useless qualities unless the coach has an ability to communicate with the players.
- A knowledgeable coach will know that the players have a variety of learning styles, also that they all learn at different rates.
- Communication should be with everyone, and the coach should employ different ways of presenting the information.
- Communication can be verbal, visual and kinaesthetic; if it is given consistently and continually reinforced, players eventually learn and performance steadily improves.
- Communication is also a two-way process and the coach should allow players to feel valued by letting them voice opinions and make suggestions.

Open-Minded and Willing to Learn

- A good coach should never stand still, there is always a question to ask and something new to learn or try. A coach who is prepared to add to their knowledge base not only increases their

England coach, Hope Powell, working with her players in a pre-game warm-up.

understanding of the whole coaching process, but also improves their own ability to deliver that knowledge.

- Open-minded coaches are prepared to listen to players, they accept that there can be other solutions and they are able to adapt to new circumstances when necessary.
- This sort of approach strengthens the rapport between the coach and the players; it leads to an increase in understanding and therefore improves performance.

England Goalkeeper Rachel Brown listens to goalkeeper coach Keith Rees.

Integrity

- As a leader of people the coach is in a position of responsibility, it's a powerful role and one that should not be abused.
- An honest coach with a consistent message will quickly earn the respect of those around them and then be able to work from a position of trust.

Well Organized

- It is the coach's responsibility to provide the structure within which the team will work. There should be long-, medium- and short-term aims supported by thorough day-to-day planning and management.
- Good planning will allow the coach to maximize the time spent with the players, ensure that the message is consistent, delivered logically and continually reinforced.

The Coaching Philosophy

Every coach has their own philosophy with regards to the game. How it should be played, how it should be coached, why they are personally involved and what they want to get out of their coaching. Their philosophy is rooted in their own personal set of values and beliefs,

A few last-minute instructions.

having been shaped over time by experiences, both in football and outside it.

As has already been stated, the role of the coach is to develop team performance and create conditions that will give the players the best chance of success. This involves shaping the environment both on and off the pitch, it affects training, travelling, meet-ups and even down-time. A good structure provides stability and develops confidence, thereby allowing the coach to deliver her message both consistently and effectively.

The type of structure put into place by the coach will reflect their personal coaching philosophy but should also consider the specific circumstances of the team being coached. For example, an under-16 youth team representing a village and playing in a local league will have different priorities from a team of the same age competing in centre of excellence football. That doesn't mean to say that the coach has to compromise her values when working with either of the teams, just adjust the message in order to fit the needs of the players.

When taking over a team, the coach needs to establish what the team's particular needs are by finding the answers to three questions:

FIFA coaching clinic with the Spanish Under-19 squad.

- What are the expectations and long-term aims of the team or club?
- How important are winning and results over the development of a team or club?
- What can be realistically achieved by the team or club, both now and in the future?

The answers set the tone for the environment and will allow the coach to work without compromise within her own philosophy. A good structure will provide reliability, unity and purpose, it will allow the coach to work methodically and create the conditions for everyone to move in the same direction.

A Player-Centred Environment

Player-centred environments put the player at the heart of the coaching process, creating conditions where they are valued and their opinions count. By giving them responsibility, they are more likely to buy into their learning and respond positively. Ultimately, players learn to make their own decisions, perform better, are more inspired and are prepared to work harder.

Player-centred environments are competitive and challenging for all concerned, but most especially the coach. The coach is now a facilitator, setting problems for the players, then providing the guidance and support necessary to help them solve those problems. Some argue that this leads to the coach's authority being undermined, but ultimately it is the more rewarding approach leading to the greater development of all.

Creating a Female Player-Centred Environment

It should be emphasized at this point that the techniques and tactics of football are the same in both the male and the female game. The information required to coach a back four to play zonally, or an individual to improve their heading skills does not vary between genders. However, what the coach should be aware of is the way that information is delivered. Not only should it be presented in a style and at a level suitable for the age and experience of the players, but it should also be adapted to suit the gender of the group. It is a fact that males and females have brain-based differences that affect their behaviour in learning environments. When teaching football this is easily overlooked because our culture defines football as a 'masculine' sport, and expects female players to behave, respond and play in the same way as their male counterparts.

It is worth noting that:

- Girls learn best in a calm, static environment, which is an ideal opportunity to create an interactive learning environment more in tune with a female learning style.
- In general, girls are more group-orientated than boys. They like instruction and are keen to learn, often motivated by a desire to please their coach. If encouraged, they will practise away from formal sessions and will also be willing to try out new ideas. These factors make female players easier to work with because they are already receptive to the coaching environment.
- The group is more important than the individual, which is a great advantage for developing team play, although this can sometimes mean that the more timid individuals 'hide' so they don't stand out from the rest. In such cases the challenge for the coach is to encourage these individuals to showcase their talent and, if anything, become more 'selfish' in possession of the ball.
- Girls are sociable and they need to be given the opportunity to chat, talk and ask questions. The coaching session should be structured to fulfil this need without affecting the quality and tempo of the practical work.
- The coach should try to employ a range of collaborative coaching styles that encourage player involvement and decision-making. Girls respond particularly well when they are given responsibility for their own development and the interactive approach will create a good working atmosphere, as well as improve team communication and cohesion.
- The coach should try to use time wisely, setting aside specific times before or after training, at the pitch side during a coaching session, whilst travelling to a game or even at the game, in order to set problems, address problems or ask questions.

SIMPLE STRATEGIES FOR EFFECTIVE COACHING

- Encourage two-way communication with all players.
- Listen.
- Reassure and provide positive feedback.
- Remain calm and controlled.
- Set high standards.
- Encourage competition.
- Leave room for fun.
- Be fair, loyal and trustworthy.
- Encourage decision-making.
- Encourage responsibility.
- Provide consistent messages.

These can vary widely from the coaching points of a particular session to codes of conduct, behaviour, team strategy, upcoming fixtures, team aims and so on.

- The coach should be aware that the dynamics within a group of females can lead to the formation of cliques, sometimes to the exclusion of the less popular members of the team. Differences can linger over long periods of time, which is a factor that can be very disruptive to the cohesion of the team.
- Social hierarchy can also determine who works together during partnered activities, a situation that does not always benefit individual development. The coach, therefore, should occasionally choose who works with whom, matching them by position, size and ability as opposed to friendships.
- Relationships are important to girls, which can mean that they may be reluctant to compete against their friends in the training environment. Social conditioning, too, can have a subconscious effect on behaviour, as aggression and competitiveness are often seen as unfeminine traits. Girls need to be reassured that it is okay to compete with their friends. They have to understand that training is a rehearsal for the game and that play should always be at a high tempo, in order to create realistic challenges and problems for them to solve.

- Girls care what others think about them and are more prone to an emotive response than boys. Their sensitivity has a direct link to their overall self-esteem and confidence. Female players, therefore, need praise and constant reassurance in order to boost their often erratic levels of confidence. The coach should provide honest and meaningful feedback on a regular basis to the group, as well as to all the individuals in the team. The words that are used should be positive and as specific as possible. It also helps to be clear about expectations by avoiding generalizations and setting both long- and short-term aims for the team.

Coaching is certainly not a case of 'one size fits all', no matter what gender the players are. To achieve success with female teams, the coach clearly needs to be aware of the differences in behaviour between gender groups and then shape the environment accordingly into one that appeals to female players. In summary this should be:

- Player-centred.
- Interactive.
- Competitive.
- Fulfilling.
- Enjoyable.

Such an environment will allow the girls to succeed in their own way and on their own terms.

Celebrating a cup final victory.

A Brief Interview with Brent Hills, Assistant Women's National Coach

Brent became the Women's National Team Assistant Coach in 2002 after three decades of work in the professional game as youth team coach at Brentford, Millwall, Watford and Fulham. As well as his duties with the women's senior team, he is charged with the task of looking after the Under-21 squad, which provides a vital stepping stone for youth international players into senior women's international football. He gained his Pro Licence in 2005, and is also a well-respected FA coach educator.

Brent Hills.

Question: You have spent many years working in football, what are the key differences between working in a male as opposed to a female environment?

Answer: In general, female players are more co-operative than the men, they like to work together and are more productive in groups. They are also willing to work at their development in a more honest way. Although I have to say that men can take criticism more robustly and seem to be more competitive, I suppose that is due in general because they are in a highly competitive environment on a day-to-day basis.

Question: Do you modify the way that you coach when you are working with female players?

Answer: Not really, although I do try to be more patient and tap into their co-operative instincts to gain success. I also try to give the players more opportunities to make their own decisions and try to be as supportive as I can. It does take longer to develop a female player because, in general, she has less practice time and fewer playing opportunities. This means that repetition is the key to success with female players, albeit with variety, so that the practices remain interesting.

Question: What are the key differences in the way women play the game as opposed to male players?

Answer: Strength and power is more of an issue with women, so that means that the range of passing is, in general, shorter and the tempo is reduced. Games are also played in a very sporting manner, despite the heat of competition, which is refreshing.

Question: Since being employed as assistant women's coach, what improvements have you observed in the way teams prepare for, and compete in, tournaments?

Answer: Everything is developing and improving, we have settled age groups and a more comprehensive games programme, supported by better monitoring of players away from the squad meet-ups. We're also scouting more and preparing our players to cope with the pressures on and off the field.

Question: What advice would you give to a new coach just starting out in the women's game?

Answer: Always strive to be as organized as you can, constantly educate yourself in all facets of coaching and always try to be the best you can.

Question: Is there anything else that you would like to add?

Answer: The game still has a huge amount of potential and its continued improvement will be driven by better qualified coaches, better facilities, professional players and more opportunities for girls to play the game in schools and clubs.

CHAPTER 4

ATTRIBUTES OF THE FEMALE PLAYER

This chapter is concerned with the player and the qualities that she needs in order to play the game. In most parts of the world, football is seen as a man's game and performance is measured using male criteria. Often, in an attempt to make people respect the women's game and thereby fit into the football community, comparisons are made between male and female players. However this is unfair and, although the two games seem the same, the style and pace of play are different. Women's football is a unique sport in its own right; the game has its own rhythm, its own personalities and its own way of doing things. It is from this angle that we should base our assessments of the female player. With our ideal female player as a starting point, the coach has more realistic expectations and is better able to develop a performance that suits his or her own team.

Profiling the Female Player

Football is a simple game to play and an entertaining game to watch; however, when it comes to defining performance, the picture becomes more complicated. It's a team game, but the team is dependent upon the qualities of each individual for the effectiveness of its performance. No two players are alike and each has a varying number of strengths and weaknesses.

By looking at the best female players, then breaking down their performance into a list of individual qualities, a profile of a perfect performance can be developed. The profile can then be used to quantify and assess the qualities of other female players. A player-profile form provides the coach with a tool that can be used to measure a player's performance, creating a snapshot and giving a base from which her future development can be planned.

Defining Performance

Technical and Tactical Qualities

These relate directly to the game, covering the player's technical ability, both on and off the ball, her game knowledge and her overall understanding of her role within the team.

Technical

Good technique is crucial for a player to be able to play the game. It doesn't matter what position she plays, or

LEFT: *Arsenal's Rachel Yankey on the ball.*

RIGHT: *Women's Premier League action between Leicester and Preston.*

PLAYER-PROFILE FORM

Technical/Tactical Notes

Core techniques	1	2	3	4	5
Technical range	1	2	3	4	5
Decision-making	1	2	3	4	5
Game understanding	1	2	3	4	5
Creativity	1	2	3	4	5

Physical

Aerobic endurance	1	2	3	4	5
Agility	1	2	3	4	5
Flexibility	1	2	3	4	5
Power	1	2	3	4	5
Speed and reaction	1	2	3	4	5
Speed endurance	1	2	3	4	5
Strength	1	2	3	4	5

Social

Relationships and interaction	1	2	3	4	5
Lifestyle management	1	2	3	4	5
Self-esteem	1	2	3	4	5

Psychological

Confidence	1	2	3	4	5
Concentration	1	2	3	4	5
Commitment	1	2	3	4	5
Communication skills	1	2	3	4	5
Control	1	2	3	4	5

Interpretation of marking system:

1	Poor
2	Significant weaknesses
3	Average for group
4	Good
5	Excellent

Ellen White celebrates a goal on her debut for the England senior team.

at what level she competes, her technical ability must be at least equal to those around her, in order to be successful.

Good technique underpins performance, although it should be noted that technique without skill is worthless. A skilful player applies her technical ability in game play. She uses her techniques to compete at pace against an opponent, success feeds her confidence, speeds up her decision-making and turns her into a more effective player.

Tactical

The team is split into units – forwards, midfield and defence – with each player having a specific role to play within that unit. Every position has both offensive and defensive responsibilities, which are defined by the tactics and strategies employed by the team.

Players need game understanding. They must have knowledge of their own role and the better they under-

CORE TECHNIQUES	
Outfield players	**Goalkeepers**
Ball mastery	Handling
Passing – long and short	Footwork
Heading	Shot stopping
Shooting	Dealing with crosses and high balls
Dribbling, turning and changing direction with the ball	Distribution – throwing and kicking
Defending in 1 v 1s and small units	

stand it, the more they are able to make good decisions in the game. An appreciation of the role of other players is also important to the overall performance of the team.

Sometimes a player is described as being able to 'read the game', which refers to a subconscious ability to anticipate what will happen, then act in accordance with the circumstances in order to influence the outcome of the game.

Physiological Qualities

This is an assessment of a player's athletic ability and her overall fitness for football.

Football is a sport where height, power and explosive movement can win or lose games. There is full contact and each game lasts for 90 minutes. All players, therefore, need a range of physical attributes in order to be competitive. During a typical game, players will walk, jog, run, sprint, jump and fall repeatedly. They require aerobic and anaerobic endurance, upper and lower body strength, agility to be able to change direction and flexibility to be able to reach, bend and stretch.

Overall, the fitness levels in the women's game have increased in the last decade, and stronger female players are producing faster-paced games, with a tempo that is sustained over 90 minutes.

Psychological Qualities

If a player is to remain competitive throughout a long and intensive game, she will need more than just physical qualities. If she is serious about her training and development, it will be her mind that forces her to work that little bit harder or longer in the pursuit of a better performance. Our ideal player, therefore, requires certain mental qualities that will supplement her technical skills and physical ability.

Mental toughness is often cited as the quality that provides the winning edge in close matches, but it can be broken down into component parts, which help us to understand what it actually is. These are control,

England's Kelly Smith on the ball.

confidence, commitment, communication, concentration and together they determine the level of the player's winning attitude.

Social Qualities

Football is a team game with many diverse characters contributing to the group. This category highlights qualities which relate to our players' ability to positively interact within the team environment. That doesn't mean that they have to be the 'life and soul' of the group, but neither should they possess destructive qualities which undermine its cohesion and upset its balance.

The Female Player in Action

The game has undergone phenomenal growth on a worldwide scale and it is interesting to observe the way that different national federations have chosen to develop their female teams and players. For some, technique is the foundation of performance and its development is stressed above all else. This has long been the example in France, where players are specifically not taught tactical play until they have mastered technique. For others, such as the United States, physical and psychological qualities assume greater importance. They have dominated women's international football since the first women's world cup in 1991, with a work ethic and an unshakeable self-confidence that is second to none. In Japan, where the national team has undergone a steady rise to prominence over the last decade, the federation has adapted its playing strategy in order to suit the physical capabilities of its players. They recognized that their teams are, on average, smaller than

England captain Faye White.

their opponents and have turned this to their advantage by combining a short, intricate passing game supported by high levels of fitness and a phenomenal work rate. Some of the best female players in the world base their entire game on their technical mastery, for others their techniques merely underpin other strengths to their game. The Brazilian striker Marta has been named FIFA

Everton and England goalkeeper, Rachel Brown.

Women's World Player of the Year an unprecedented four times, in 2006, 2007, 2008 and 2009. With the ball at her feet, her talents are mesmerizing, but it is an electric change of pace and a single-minded pursuit of the goal that gives her that world-class edge over defenders. Closer to home, another world-class striker is England's Kelly Smith. Like Marta she has excellent technical ability, a talent for beating defenders and an eye for goal, but she differs in the way she works with her team to create opportunities for others as well as herself. Birgit Prinz, the German forward, gained a lot of her success because of her physical prowess. She made her full international debut at the age of sixteen back in 1994, and even then her height, strength and speed set her apart from her peers. Since then she has had a consistent and highly successful career, being voted FIFA's Women's Player of the Year for three consecutive years from 2003 to 2005.

There is a variety of playing positions and roles in any one team. It is obvious that goalkeepers and outfield players require a very different set of technical qualities, but it should also be understood that each outfield position has subtle variations in its technical emphasis.

To be more specific, wide midfielders are expected to beat players, either in the dribble or through good movement. They should be able to deliver effective crosses or passes into danger areas in the last third of the field. Central defenders, on the other hand, are expected to dominate one-on-one situations. They should be able to pressurize quickly and effectively, as well as compete in the air. England international Faye White has excellent all-round qualities, making her one of the most dominant central defenders in the world. Following the Women's World Cup in China in 2007, she was selected for the same all-star team as Marta, but for very different reasons. She has a good physique, well-suited to a central role, whilst her temperament is ideal for calm and thoughtful defensive play. Her positioning in relation to the ball, along with decisive movement to pressurize or win the ball, makes her a formidable opponent to play against. Once in possession, she is confident and has a range of passing techniques that allows her to initiate and support her team's attacking moves.

Goalkeeping is an area in which the female game has made the biggest strides in recent years. It stands to

England Women line up before a world-cup qualifying game.

reason that women, playing in the same-sized goals as men, are going to find it more difficult to 'fill' the goal because, on average, they are both smaller and of a slighter build. Positioning off the goal line is most crucial for the female goalkeeper because of her height in relation to the size of the goal, but angles and distances from the ball are also important. Female goalkeepers also need to think about, and develop, their 'presence' within the team, especially when there is no specialized goalkeeping coach, as they can be easily overlooked by the already overworked team coach. An aspiring goalkeeper or goalkeeper coach would do well to look to Germany for two of the best female goalkeepers in recent years, Silke Rottenburg and Nadine Angerer. Between them they have played over 200 times for their country and have both carved out formidable reputations. Despite both being less than 6ft (2m) tall they dominate their goal through their sheer presence, working on and off the goal line with ease. Their obvious technical excellence, total concentration and vociferous support spread confidence and provide an excellent platform from which the team can build its performance.

The Importance of Female Role Models

For a young or an inexperienced player having a role model is one important way to find the motivation to improve her game. Watching great players, male and female, provides visual images of their skills, giving the youngster something tangible to emulate. When these players happen to be female, the message is not only more realistic but more powerful.

In the USA, participation in girls' soccer is massive; the international programme is arguably the best in the world and there is a women's professional league, which attracts players from around the world. Because of these factors, football has a slightly more feminine profile than elsewhere and each new generation of female players has the achievements of the last to inspire them. For many, Mia Hamm was considered to be the best female player in the world, during a playing career that spanned seventeen years from 1987 to 2004. Overall she played 275 times for her country and scored 158 goals, representing the USA in four World Cup competitions and three Olympic competitions. During her career she became an inspiration and role model not only to female football players, but to a whole generation of sports-minded girls throughout the United States of America. Her example illustrates how the women's game can be developed through the use

Karen Carney.

of appropriate personalities to act as role models for the upcoming generation.

Elsewhere in the world, where women's football receives considerably less media exposure, the use of role models can play a key role in the promotion of the game as being one suitable for females. FIFA has recognized this and appointed fifteen former players to be their ambassadors for the game worldwide. On a more local level, development can be sustained by promoting the achievements of female players associated with the region.

In the UK, the women's game has made tremendous strides over the last twenty years and newcomers to women's football have some excellent home-grown talent to look to for their inspiration. There has been a great emphasis placed on youth development during this time and many of the young players coming into the game took their motivation from the achievements of Kelly Smith. She has been the most high-profile English

Eniola Aluko.

player of the last decade, achieving success as a professional player in America, as well as on the international stage. Now that her path has been followed by young players, such as Karen Carney and Eniola Aluko, both of whom are now international team-mates as well as professionals playing in America, the stage is set for continued development and sustained growth.

Conclusions

Football is a global game with a huge media profile. In the past, female players never had a shortage of male personalities to emulate, but now they can look to some excellent examples in their own game. There are more opportunities than ever before for the female player to play and it's exciting to think that women's football can finally stand on its own feet, that it can build on its own history and traditions to create a game that is not only skilful to watch but highly entertaining too.

A Brief Interview with Karen Carney, England International and Professional Player

Karen was a typical sports-mad youngster, who began playing organized football at the age of eleven and went on to play in the women's premier league for Birmingham City and Arsenal, before heading across the Atlantic to become a professional with the Chicago Red Stars. She is an established England international, making her debut for the senior team in the 2005 European Championships at the age of eighteen.

Question: What is your background in sport?

Answer: At school I did every sport possible: badminton, cross-country, hockey, you name it I did it. I was even a dancer too. Then it became a choice and, although I enjoyed dancing, I was better at football and knew I could go far. In the end it was easy to choose.

Question: Who are your biggest influences?

Answer: My parents and sisters have been great to me, they are my backbone and whether I win or lose, play good or bad, they are always there for me. They are great role models for me too. Another person would be Marcus Bignot, my first coach at Birmingham. I think I inherited his love of the game. We speak all the time, he's part of my family.

Question: Does it make a difference being coached by a male coach as opposed to a female coach?

Answer: I honestly don't think it matters. I've been coached by both males and females. There are some differences but really if you're a good coach, it doesn't matter what gender you are. Your methods will always be able to get your athletes to respond and play to their best.

Question: What is your biggest achievement in football to date?

Answer: Definitely playing for my country and also winning the UEFA Cup with Arsenal. I love playing for my country; you just can't beat that feeling.

Question: What are your aims in football?

Answer: With Chicago I want to win the WPS so much. Internationally, it's got to be to qualify for the next World Cup and then kick on from there.

Question: What are the differences between playing in the USA and playing in England?

Answer: In England, the game is more technical and probably more skilful. In the USA, it's faster and more physical but I love the challenge playing against the best players in the world.

Karen Carney.

Every week I know I'm in a game and that if I make one mistake I'll get punished.

Question: Talk us through a typical day as a professional footballer.

Answer: Well, at the moment it's pre-season and I'm on rehab, so it's a bit different.

Question: Have you any advice to give someone just starting out in the game?

Answer: Just enjoy it and have fun, you play your best when you're happy and there are no expectations. Also listen, listen and listen, that way you will learn.

Question: What hopes do you have for the future of women's football?

Answer: Here in the USA I'd like to see the professional league get stronger, with bigger crowds and more teams. In England, I hope the same happens and we get a professional summer league. For the game, I just want to see it grow so girls like me can have a chance to play professionally at a sport they love.

CHAPTER 5

TECHNICAL FOUNDATIONS

Good technical ability is essential if a player is to perform well under game conditions. Techniques are normally learnt at a young age and then reinforced throughout the playing career. When introducing a new technique, practice should be unpressured so that the player can learn the movement pattern, then, over time, challenges can be introduced to speed up her execution of the technique.

When a player's techniques have become second nature and are performed consistently well under pressure from opponents, then the player can be said to have developed her technique into a skill.

There are five core techniques that an outfield player should develop and, although she may have a certain amount of natural talent, practice is the key to any real or lasting improvements in her performance. The practice should be realistic, varied and progressive, relating always to the age, understanding and ability of the players.

The five techniques covered in this chapter are:

- Ball mastery.
- Passing.
- Running, dribbling and turning with the ball.
- Heading.
- Shooting and finishing.

SIMPLE STRATEGIES TO MAXIMIZE DEVELOPMENT

The message for the player is simple, learn how to do it then:

- Practise, practise, practise.
- Add challenge into the practice.
- Be prepared for failure at first.
- Persevere.
- Do it quicker.
- Repeat.

LEFT: Reaching to make a quality first touch.

The Training Session

The skills of the coach lie in how they shape the environment in order to inspire the player, but it is the player who ultimately determines the quality of the practical work. The key to developing a skilful performance is based on the individual repetition of the correct technique over a period of time, the more familiar a player becomes with the correct movement patterns that are associated with each technique the quicker she will be able to execute them.

Format for Practice

Time

The length of time that the players practise is important and more is not necessarily better. The aim instead should be consistency, correct practice and high quality at all times. Depending on the age of the players, the training sessions should last for between 60 and 90 minutes, and be structured to provide a number of stimulating activities throughout the session. Working in a short burst of interesting activity will ensure maximum concentration, keep the intensity of the practical elements high and prevent boredom.

A typical 90-minute training session could be organized in the following manner:

- Coach arrives early to set up the training area and is ready to greet the players at the start of the session.
- Players are encouraged to arrive early. This mainly has a social purpose, but the time can also be used as informal practice time, which will help to focus the players' minds on the session to come.
- Warm-up – 20 minutes approximately.
- Technical activity – 15 minutes approximately.
- Technical activity progression – 20 minutes approximately.
- Small-sided game – 20 minutes approximately.
- Cool down and debrief – 10 minutes approximately.
- Cumulative total for drinks breaks – 5 minutes approximately.

Faye White and Casey Stoney practising simple techniques during an England pre-game warm-up.

Professionalism

A professional approach is a metaphor for a focused and determined mindset. It is one that takes responsibility seriously and works hard in order to deliver results.

A professional approach applies equally to players and coaches, but initially stems from the environment that is created by the coach. It is the coach who sets the standards and creates the conditions that will determine the extent to which the players focus on their training. Then it is up to the players to respond not only by meeting those expectations, but also exceeding them, wherever possible.

Organization

Organization is a key factor in ensuring a consistent approach over the course of time. A session planned in advance will flow from one activity into the next, not only making it easy to manage, but also maximizing the time that the players spend doing what they like best, which is playing. The coach should consider the following when planning a session.

Facilities

The type, size and layout of the facility will determine the way a session is structured. For example, an indoor session in a small gym, planning to focus on finishing, should be very different from one set up outside on a full-sized grass pitch.

Equipment

The coach should consider what equipment is available and then use it to enhance the quality of the session.

Ideally there should be enough footballs for one per player, as well as an abundance of cones, bibs and goals to mark areas, set out targets and create teams.

Number of Players

As well as being able to utilize the available space, a coach must also know how to organize the players effectively and realistically within that space. A coach should be able to adapt to large or small groups, odd numbers, as well as unexpected absences or injury.

Maximizing Time on the Ball

At the start of this chapter it was stated that correct practice and repetition lead to the development of performance. Therefore, the way a coach handles the number of players and space in which they work will have a significant impact on their progress. Players should be organized into small groups for repetitive, high-tempo practice, rather than standing in long lines waiting for their turn. The size of the areas used for the practice should be carefully considered and matched to both the age and the players' level of experience.

For example:

- Large areas will allow time on the ball and therefore create good conditions for success, but the coach should also consider the distances involved in the area. Having to run further or pass over longer distances could prove to be physically demanding for the players. It could quickly lead to fatigue and consequently cause the quality of the practice to suffer.
- Smaller areas will restrict the amount of space available making the practice faster and more challenging. The coach must observe carefully, is it

Open play during a Linby Ladies training session.

realistic, is the quality being maintained and, most importantly, are the players achieving success? If so, the players are gaining valuable practice and developing their game; if not, the area needs to be adapted to suit the needs of the players.

Challenging All Players

The challenge should be realistic, linked to the specific needs of the group, as well as the individuals within the group. For beginners, that can be as simple as setting out an area in which a simple technique can be practised, or for the more experienced group, by adding pressure through time conditions or introducing opposition and directional play. The duration of a specific activity is also an important consideration because practices that are too pressured for too long lead to fatigue and will cause the quality to drop.

Practise at a High Tempo

With so many things to thing about it is easy for the coach to forget that the training session is merely a rehearsal for the game and, although there is no substitute for correct, repetitive practice, the tempo of a training session also has a vital role to play in the development of performance. Practical work should almost always be undertaken at match pace and our female players educated to understand that it is okay to compete with, and against, each other.

Set a Theme

A well-organized and planned session will have a simple theme, with specific coaching points and an expected outcome. The information should be delivered consistently and concisely throughout the session and using a style of communication that is appropriate to the age group being coached.

Let the Game be the Teacher

Effective communication can vary enormously from coach to coach, but undoubtedly, when verbal instruction is kept simple and to a minimum the practice will flow, the players will work harder and learning will be taking place. It is far more inspirational to be active than it is to be standing in the cold listening to the coach, or waiting in line for a turn. In addition, if the practice is structured to allow the players to play, then they will be learning to make their own decisions and therefore taking responsibility for their own development.

Developing Essential Techniques

Note:

- Each essential technique is defined in the following pages.
- There are suggestions in the text for individual, as well as squad, development.
- Session plans are sized for groups of twelve adult players, but can easily be adapted for younger or less experienced players by adjusting the area sizes.
- The session plans are meant merely to be a starting point and by no means the definitive way in which to teach and develop technique.
- Every session included in this book has been used thoroughly with many different groups of players and has been chosen for inclusion due to its effectiveness with those players.

Ball Mastery

Definition
Ball mastery is an ability to bring the ball under control as quickly as possible. It involves using any permitted part of the body and taking as few touches as possible. Ball mastery can also be referred to as first touch.

Why is it Fundamental?
A player who has a good first touch and can master the ball is in control, not only of the particular situation in the game, but also of herself. When the position of the ball becomes second nature, the player is confident. She is able to assess the situation and think about her options before making a decision.

Players at all levels should strive for high quality in their first touch and continually work to improve it throughout their playing career.

Individual Development

Players require different techniques to allow them to control the ball, no matter whether it is on the ground or in the air. To be able to develop these they must be familiar with the ball and able to 'feel' it at their feet. Ball-juggling and ball-manipulation exercises are two simple ways to promote this, with each being well-suited to individual practice and development.

Leicester's Natasha Meade takes an excellent first touch whilst moving at pace.

Players should be shown how to do these exercises and encouraged to have their own ball, so that they can practise them away from the formal sessions. The more time a player spends one-to-one with the ball, the more familiar she will become. Any small area can be utilized for practising juggling and manipulation, whilst walls make great rebound surfaces for working on first touch on the move or on the turn.

Ball Juggling
Keeping the ball in the air is a challenge that few players can resist and many spend hours perfecting their tricks and techniques. Ball juggling involves getting the ball into the air and then keeping it there by controlling it with either foot or thigh, the chest or the head. It is a perfect activity to set 'homework' challenges for players, as every touch means that they are developing their own unique affinity with the ball. However, it is also important to remember that everyone has their own level. Weaker players, especially youngsters, can easily be discouraged when only the best performers in the group are highlighted. Ball juggling can also be included as an activity in a more formal coaching session.

The player is in a balanced position with her eyes on the ball.

Keeping the ball in the air using the foot.

Keeping the ball in the air using the thigh.

Keeping the ball in the air using the head.

Typical ball-juggling challenges include the following.

Working Individually
- Ask players to find different ways of flicking the ball into the air. Beginners can be allowed to use their hands.
- Once the ball is in the air, challenge each player to double the number of touches that they use to keep it there. For example, beginners might only be able to keep the ball off the ground for one touch, therefore challenge them to make it two, then four and so on.
- More proficient players can be challenged to use both feet, both thighs or to keep the ball in the air by using each controlling surface in a specific order.

Working in Pairs or Small Groups
- Each player takes it in turns to keep the ball in the air. To make the practice easier, one bounce could be allowed.
- One player juggles the ball, keeping it in the air, whilst the other provides pressure by trying to challenge for the ball.
- The players take it in turns to serve the ball across the area to each other. As the ball travels they specify which surface their partner should use for the initial contact on the ball. (This could be as specific as left thigh or right foot, or a more general call of foot or thigh.).
- An alternative to the previous exercise, the serving player would call out a number as the ball travels. This means that the receiver must keep the ball in the air for that number of touches.

Teaching Points
- Balanced and co-ordinated. The player should not reach for the ball.
- Eyes on the ball.
- Keep movements small and fluid.
- Relax on contact with the ball, cushion it to prevent it bouncing away.

The photographs on page 49 illustrate good practice. In each image the player is relaxed and entirely focused on the ball. Her arms are spread to provide balance and her legs are bent to ensure cushioned control on contact.

Ball Manipulation
Players should be encouraged to use both feet and try different techniques so that they learn to move easily with the ball. There are a number of simple

Ball manipulation – rolls.

Ball manipulation – toe taps.

manipulation exercises to help to develop a sure touch. As with ball juggling these are easily practised away from formal sessions, or incorporated into warm-up and other technical activities.

Ball manipulation can be incorporated into formal warm-ups, technical sessions and cool downs. Players can also be encouraged to practise informally during drink breaks and down-time.

- Drags. The foot is rolled over the top of the ball to move it backwards. Alternate feet are used.
- Rolls. The foot is rolled over the top of the ball to move it forwards. Alternate feet are used.
- Sideways rolls. The foot is rolled across the top of the ball to move it across the body to the left or right. Alternate feet are used.
- Toe taps. The player jumps over the ball, tapping the top of it with the sole of her foot. She alternates feet and remains in a stationary position.

Teaching Points
- Balance and co-ordination.
- The ball should remain close to the feet.
- The head should be up with the eyes scanning the area. She shouldn't look at the ball.
- Movements should be small and fluid.
- The player should be light on her feet.
- Both feet should be used equally.

Ball Mastery in the Warm-Up
The coach can use these activities in a formal setting and involve the whole squad, including the goalkeepers.

Unopposed Ball Manipulation
Every player has a ball each and moves freely around a marked area. The smaller the area, the more the player has to keep the ball close to her feet. She will also take more touches to keep the ball close and will have to look around to assess where there is space.

Conditions imposed by the coach to encourage development include:

- The player stops the ball with a specified part of their body, then moves away to find another one.
- Two players make eye contact, communicate verbally and then pass their ball to the other.
- Some players in the group have no ball and are to act as passive defenders in order to force awareness and close control.

Simple Receiving
This should be a larger area than above in order to provide enough space to work freely. The players work in pairs with a ball between two and move around the area passing it between each other.

The player's first touch should not stop the ball; instead she should control it into an adjacent space. This could be in front of the player or sideways, left or right or even involve a turn. Her second touch should be the pass back to her partner.

Encourage players to use both feet and to take the controlling first touch with the inside, outside and laces of the foot.

As a development the coach can progress on to one-touch passing, which requires precision and high quality.

Group Development

Simple squad practices to develop ball mastery, first touch and ball control are outlined in the following practices.

Practice 1

Skill level – beginners.

Purpose
To practise ball mastery and first touch with the ball on the ground.

Number of Players
Whole squad.

Size of Area
- Overall size: 40 × 30 yards.
- Inner area size: 20 × 10 yards.

Type of Session
Could be used as a warm-up for technically competent players of all ages, or a technical-development session for less experienced players.

Timing
Can vary according to the session type, but it should normally last for no more than 15 minutes, unless there are progressions.

Organization
- Split the group into two. Each team doesn't have to contain equal numbers.
- One group has a ball each and works inside the inner area.
- The other group spread themselves out around the outside of the larger area.
- The players with the ball maintain close control inside the central marked area, but look for opportunities to make a pass to a player on the outside. After the pass, she moves into the neutral zone and takes up a good position to receive the return pass from the outside.
- The player on the outside receives the ball and controls it on her first touch. She now has a choice:

  She can make the return pass on her second touch OR

Carry the ball into the central area to work on her own ball mastery techniques.
If the latter happens, the red player exchanges roles with the blue player on the outside of the outside area.

Teaching Points
General good practice:
- Players should show awareness in all roles, playing with their head up and scanning for space and opportunity.
- Players should be light on their feet and working on their toes.
- The tempo of the practice should be high-paced.

Central area:
- Keep the ball close, practise with all parts of each foot.
- Before passing the ball, the player must communicate with a receiver on the outer area. This is by eye contact and also verbally.

Outer area receiving player:
- Get into line with the moving ball after it is passed.
- Take a good first touch to one side using the outside, inside or laces of either foot.
- The ball should not be stopped.

Suggested Progressions and Challenges
- If the player on the outer area decides to pass back to the player in the neutral zone, allow her to pick up the ball and throw it back for aerial control. (Or if playing standards allow the ball can be chipped back.)
- The player in the neutral zone follows the pass and forces the player on the outside to swap roles. This will also put the player under pressure when receiving the ball, forcing a good first touch into space away from the pressuring player.
- One or two players can be given defensive duties in the central area. They will either be conditioned to offer passive pressure to the players on the ball or be given full opportunity to win the ball.

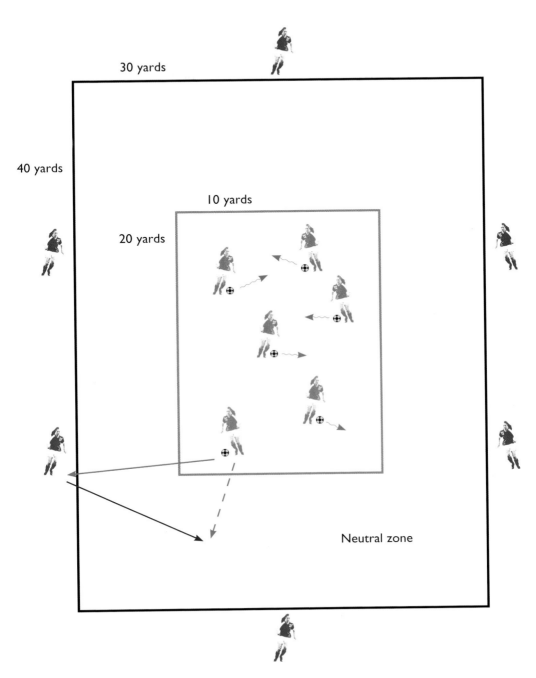

30 yards

40 yards

10 yards

20 yards

Neutral zone

Practice 1 – ball mastery.

Practice 2

Skill level – intermediate.

Purpose
To practise first touch with the ball on the ground and in the air.

Number of Players
Whole squad.

Size of Area
* Overall size: 40 × 30 yards.
* End zone: 15 × 30 yards.
* Middle zone: 10 × 30 yards.

Type of Session
A technical-development session for players of all abilities, although please note that, due to the introduction of longer passes, the quality and flow of the practice, when it is undertaken with less-experienced players, could be disrupted.

Timing
The duration of the practice should be at least 20 to 25 minutes.

Organization
* The group is split into three teams. If numbers are unequal, try to balance each team in relation to playing ability.
* Each team is to work inside one of the three zones, as marked on the diagram on page 55.
* The aim of the game is to pass the ball from end to end without the team in the middle intercepting.
* After receiving a long pass from the other end zone, the receiver should play a short pass to a team-mate in the same end zone.
* The coach should be positioned centrally outside the playing area with all the spare balls. This will help to maintain the tempo of the practice, as a new ball can be immediately served into the practice when the one in use is overhit or miscontrolled.
* After the team in the middle zone has intercepted the ball a pre-determined number of times, they exchange places with a team in one of the end zones.

Teaching Points
General good practice:
* Players should show awareness in all roles, playing with their head up and scanning for space and opportunity.
* Players should be light on their feet and working on their toes.
* The tempo of the practice should be high-paced.

End-zone receivers:
* Move into the line of the ball as it is passed from the other end zone.
* The receiver should adjust her position to take her first controlling touch on the ball as early as possible.
* As the ball travels, the receiver decides how to control the ball and what surface to use.
* Relax on contact.
* The ball should be cushioned and controlled into a nearby space.

Suggested Progressions and Challenges
* As the ball travels from one end zone into the other, one or more player(s) from the middle zone are allowed to move into the end zone to pressurize the receivers, turning the game in the end zone into a 4 v 1 or 4 v 2.
* The pressure can be conditioned to be passive or full 'pressure' and the movement of the middle-zone players into the end zone can be restricted:
  * Movement by the players in the middle zone is allowed when the ball is kicked or the moment when the receiver makes her first touch.
* After the ball has been passed to the other end zone, the defending players must move back into the middle and the practice starts again.

30 yards

15 yards

End zone

10 yards

Coaching position

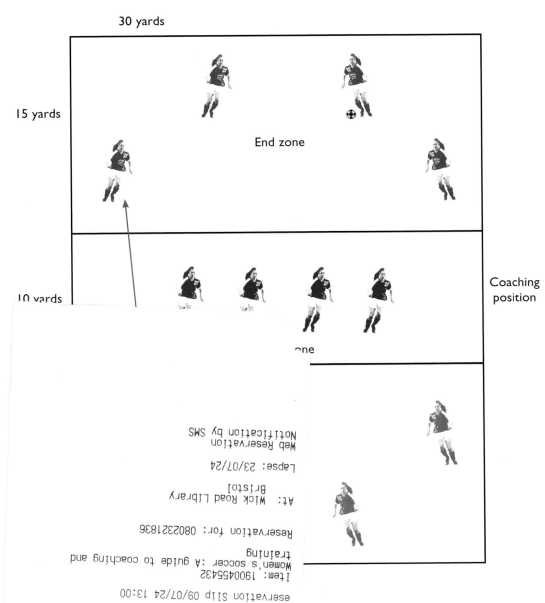

Passing

Definition

Moving the ball accurately between members of the same team in order to retain possession and build an effective attacking move.

Why is it Fundamental?

In the game of football, all teams have one simple aim – to score more goals than the other in order to win. To create goal-scoring opportunities they have to move the ball down the pitch into their opponents' defending third and, therefore, being able to pass the ball effectively over both long and short distances gives them an advantage over the opposition. Essentially, a team that can pass the ball accurately has the technical ability to control the game.

As the ball moves around the pitch, the opposition continually has to adjust position in order to defend against it. Therefore, the team that is able to employ a variety of passing techniques, executed accurately and at pace, will increase their match-winning capability.

- When developing passing techniques, players should never be totally static and the ball should rarely come to a complete standstill.
- Decision-making should be part of the practice and the coach must understand that passing is not just about keeping possession.
- Players should be educated to take calculated offensive risks, looking to play the ball forward, especially when it can be passed behind one or many members of the opposition.

Individual Development

Basic Techniques for Passing the Ball on the Ground

Push Pass

This is the most commonly used passing technique primarily because it is the easiest to learn. Contact is with the large area of the inside of the foot, ensuring the greatest chance of accuracy. The drawback to the push

Katie Chapman demonstrating the push pass, despite the close attentions of the Sunderland defender.

Foot placement for the push pass.

Foot placement for the driven pass.

pass is that it is primarily used over short distances, very predictable and lacking in pace.

Teaching Points
- The non-kicking foot is planted next to the ball with the toes facing in the direction that the ball is to be passed.
- The kicking foot is firm and strikes through the middle of the back of the ball to 'push' it along the ground to the receiving player.
- The body should be balanced and the head steady over the ball. Initially the player scans for the intended target but at the moment of contact between the foot and the ball, her eyes must be looking at the ball.
- A good follow-through with the kicking leg will ensure a pass of pace and accuracy.

Driven Pass
This is a more difficult technique because contact on the ball is via the smaller area on top of the foot, often described as the 'laces.' When executed correctly, the ball moves accurately and with a much greater pace towards its intended target, than with a push pass. Such a pass is easier to disguise, provides power and can be used effectively over all distances, it is also a technique that can be used on the run without affecting a player's stride pattern.

Teaching Points
- The approach to the ball is at a slight angle and generally requires a short run-up.
- The non-kicking foot is planted a few inches away from the side of the ball with the toes facing in the direction that the ball is to be passed.

- The kicking foot is firm with the toes pointing down towards the ground. Contact is with the 'laces' through the middle of the back of the ball.
- The body should be balanced and the head steady over the ball. Initially the player scans for the intended target but at the moment of contact between the foot and the ball her eyes must be looking at the ball.
- A good follow-through in the direction of the pass will ensure pace and accuracy.

Passing with the Outside of the Foot
The outside of the foot can be used to make a short, flicked pass or a longer swerving pass played into the path of a moving team-mate. The flicked pass is used over short distances and in tight situations; it is easily disguised and requires the minimum amount of foot movement. The longer swerving pass is more difficult to perfect but can be made on the run without breaking stride.

Teaching Points
- The non-kicking foot is planted behind and a little to the side of the ball with the toes facing in the direction that the player is moving.
- The body is balanced with the head up.
- The kicking foot is positioned inside the ball with contact being made with the outside of the foot through the middle of the side of the ball.

Either
- the foot flicks the ball in the direction of the pass by rotation outwards and away from the body; follow-through is minimal

or

Foot placement for the flicked pass.

- the foot drives the ball in the direction of the pass with a firm ankle and there is a good follow-through.

Basic Techniques for Passing the Ball in the Air

Long, Lofted Passes

Long passes increase the range over which a team can pass the ball. Typical techniques would be lofted balls played into space behind the defence and driven-forward balls for an attacking player to control. Contact on the ball can be made with the inside, outside or instep (laces) of the foot in order to impart swerve or pace to the pass.

Arsenal's Kim Little shows perfect balance as she prepares to make a long, forward pass.

Teaching Points

- Approach to the ball is at a slight angle with a short run-up. The non-kicking foot is planted behind and a little to the side of the ball.
- The body should be balanced but slightly leaning back with the head steady over the ball.
- Initially, the player scans for the intended target, but at the moment of contact between the foot and the ball, her eyes must be looking at the ball.
- The kicking foot is firm and able to swing freely.
- Contact is made through the middle of the bottom-half of the back of the ball in order to lift it off the ground.
- There is a good follow-through.

Group Development

Standard Teaching Points

The following teaching points are standard to all passing technique practices.

- Accuracy. Vital if the team is to maintain possession. It can mean a ball passed to the right or left foot or into space for a team-mate to run on to.
- Weight. The ball should neither be under-hit nor over-hit. Players should be encouraged to pass at a pace that will ensure the ball is not intercepted

---

SIMPLE GUIDELINES WHEN PRACTISING PASSING TECHNIQUES

- Never be static.
- Work on your toes.
- Play with your head up so that you can scan the pitch and make quick decisions.
- Pass accurately.
- Pass with pace.
- Practise at home, either with a friend or using a suitable wall.

---

and at one which they themselves would be able to receive and control comfortably.
- Communication. This is an essential element of any successful pass. The players involved in the pass should make eye contact (unless it is a disguised flick) and then communicate either verbally or non-verbally through body shape and pointing.
- Disguise. A player who is comfortable on either her right or left foot and has a range of techniques at her disposal should be encouraged to disguise her passing intentions by faking or pointing to pass in one direction and then flicking the ball elsewhere.

Squad Practices to Develop a Range of Passing Techniques

Practice 3

Skill level – beginners.

Purpose
To practise short-passing techniques in a realistic area.

Number of Players
Whole squad including goalkeepers, if available.

Size of Area
- Overall size: 55 × 40 yards.
- End-zone size: 20 × 40 yards.

Type of Session
A technical-development practice that is suitable for players of all ages and abilities. It could be used as a warm-up exercise, an extended technical-development session for less-experienced players or an introduction to Practice 4.

Timing
Can vary according to the session type, but it should normally last for no more than 15 minutes, unless there are progressions.

Organization
- The squad is split into two teams. Each team does not have to contain equal numbers.
- Each team is to work inside the marked end zone, with half the number of balls to players.
- The aim of the practice is to make short passes to team-mates who don't have a ball.
- The coach should be positioned centrally between each of the playing areas with a number of spare balls, in order to be able to see and work with both groups.

Teaching Points
General good practice:
- Players should play with their head up scanning for, and then moving into, the spaces.
- Players should be light on their feet and working on their toes.
- The tempo of the practice should be high-paced and players should never be static.
- The coach should insist on quality at all times.

Passing technique:
- Accuracy.
- Weight.
- Communication. It is good practice for players to communicate with the receiver before making the pass.
- Technique. Fine-tune the relevant passing technique as problems are observed.
- Disguise.

Suggested Progressions and Challenges
- Encourage players to practise with their weaker foot.
- Limit all or some players to one or two touches in order to speed up their play and decision-making.
- Reduce the area size to compress the space.
- Make one or more players defenders creating a 5 v 1 / 4 v 2 / 3 v 3 situation. Adjust the area size if necessary to make the play challenging and realistic. Defenders can be conditioned to provide either passive or full pressure. The coach should also reduce the number of balls at this point in order to create conditions that allow success for the team in possession. The coach should dictate when the defenders and passing players alternate, as this will ensure that all players get a good chance to practise their passing whilst being pressured by a defender. Finally, the defenders need motivation to win the ball as it can be demoralizing to work hard to win it only to see it given straight back to the other team, therefore:
  - the defenders should try to keep it for a set number of passes or
  - they should be provided with a target for them to work the ball through.

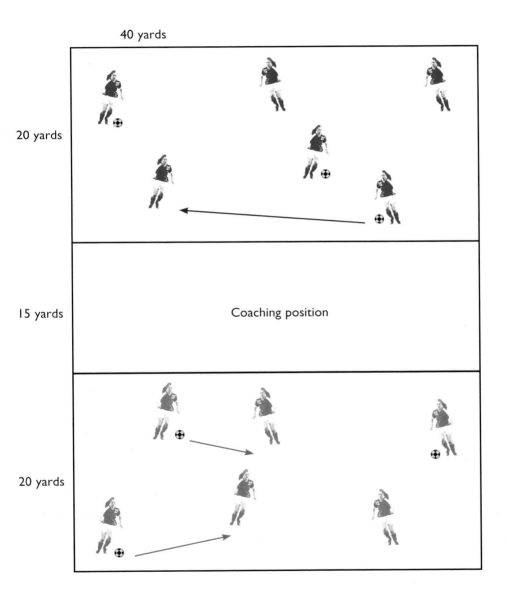

40 yards

20 yards

15 yards

Coaching position

20 yards

Practice 3 – short-passing techniques.

Practice 4

Skill level – beginners, intermediate.

Purpose
To practise short- and long-passing techniques in a realistic area.

Number of Players
Whole squad, including goalkeepers, if available.

Size of Area
- Overall size: 55 × 40 yards.
- Neutral zone: 15 × 40 yards.
- End-zone size: 20 × 40 yards.

Type of Session
A technical-development practice that is suitable for players of all ages and abilities. It should not be used as a warm-up due to the long passing element, but can be a simple progression from Practice 3, or delivered as a stand-alone session.

Timing
20 minutes.

Organization
- The squad is split into two teams working in separate areas. Each team does not have to contain equal numbers.
- Each team is to work inside the marked end zone, with half the number of balls to players.
- The aim of the practice is to pass to players without a ball in either of the end zones.
- When players play a long pass into the other end zone they must follow it and join the group who are working in that end zone.
- When a player receives a long pass, her next pass must be a short one.
- Both groups should maintain the same number of players and balls that they started with. Therefore, if a long pass is made by one group, the other group should also make a long pass to keep the same organization for the practice. This encourages players to scan and work with their heads up.

Balance on the turn in a U23 international between the USA and Sweden.

- The coach should be positioned centrally outside each of the playing areas with a number of spare balls in order to keep the practice flowing should a ball be mis-controlled or overhit.

Teaching Points

General good practice:
- Players should play with their head up, scanning for, and then moving into, the spaces.
- Players should be light on their feet and working on their toes.
- The tempo of the practice should be high-paced and players should never be static.
- The coach should insist on quality at all times.

Passing technique:
- Accuracy.
- Weight.
- Communication. It is good practice for players to communicate with the receiver before making the pass.
- Technique. Fine-tune the relevant passing technique as problems are observed.
- Disguise.

Cristen Press of the USA poised to control a difficult ball.

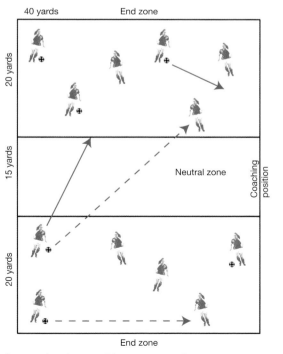

Practice 4 – short- and long-passing techniques.

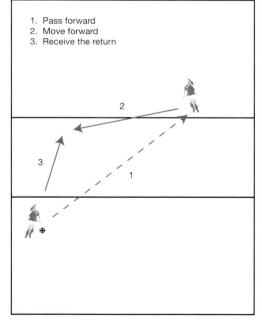

Forward passing and movement to receive the return.

Suggested Progressions and Challenges

- Encourage players to practise with their weaker foot.
- Limit all or some players to one or two touches, in order to speed up their play and decision-making.
- When players play the long 'forward' pass and then follow the pass to join the other group, they should be encouraged to receive a one-touch return from the player that they have passed to.
- Add in defenders to add pressure to the practice. These can be passive or semi-passive and located either in the neutral zone or within the end-zone playing area. The defenders should also be given targets so that there is purpose and motivation to win the ball.

RIGHT: Danni Bird plays a simple pass despite the close attentions of American defender Keelin Winters.

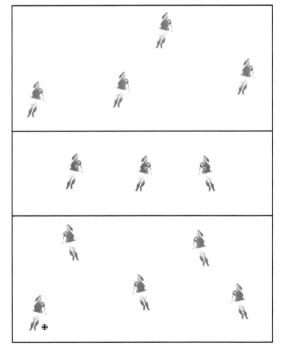

Practice 4 adapted to employ defenders in the neutral zone.

Practice 4 adapted to employ defenders in either end zone.

England U23 captain Sophie Bradley puts in a touch challenge.

American U23 midfielder Cristen Press attacks the space

England midfielder Dannielle Buet.

Practice 5

Skill level – intermediate, advanced.

Purpose

An opposed passing practice in a realistic area and with the ultimate aim of taking a shot at goal.

Number of Players

Whole squad including goalkeepers.

Size of Area

- Overall size: 55 × 40 yards.
- Neutral zone: 15 × 40 yards.
- End zone: 20 × 40 yards.

A goal has been added 10 yards outside either end zone.

Type of Session

A skills-development practice that can also be a progression from Practice 4. By including goalkeepers the whole squad is able to practise forward passing and decision-making in a structured but realistic environment.

Timing

20 minutes.

Organization

- The squad is split into two equal teams, with a goalkeeper in each team.
- Each team is split into defenders and attackers, who are located in each end zone.
- The aim of the practice is to pass the ball from the defensive end zone into the attacking end zone, finishing with a shot at goal.
- The goals are located 10 yards outside each end zone. Only the goalkeeper can use this area.
- Any player from the team who has possession of the ball can move into the central zone to receive a pass. The player will then continue her forward movement and join in with play in the attacking zone.
- Players in the central zone cannot be challenged, nor can they shoot.
- Once possession is lost, the team must regain its shape as quickly as possible (the starting formation in each end zone).
- The coach should be positioned centrally outside the playing area with a number of spare balls to maintain the momentum of the practice when the ball goes out of play.

- There should be spare balls at either end adjacent to the goal.

Teaching Points

General good practice

- Players should show awareness in all roles, playing with their head up scanning for space and opportunity.
- The tempo of the practice should be at match pace

Passing technique:

- Accuracy.
- Weight.
- Communication. It is good practice for players to communicate with the receiver before making the pass.
- Technique. Fine-tune the relevant passing technique as problems are observed.
- Disguise.

Attacking play:

- Create space. The team in possession should spread out wide and 'long', making the area as big as possible.
- Decision-making. What is the best passing option available to the player on the ball?
- Patience. The team in possession should keep play simple, generally playing off limited touches and in the direction that the player faces. The player essentially has two passing choices to make:
  - Can she play a forward pass to penetrate across the central zone into the attacking zone?
  - Can she play a shorter pass in order to keep possession and give the ball to team-mate who has more space and time?

Suggested Progressions and Challenges

- Encourage the players to work with either foot, as well as to vary the passing techniques.
- Limit some players for some of the playing time to one or two touches in order to challenge them.

COACHING TIP

When coaching open play in a small-sided game, the temptation is to provide too much information, which often deviates from the specific topic. Try to keep the coaching points simple, to the point and specific.

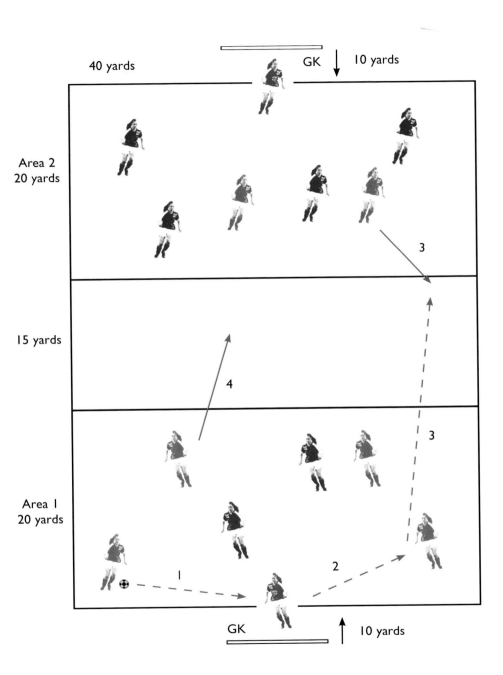

40 yards

GK 10 yards

Area 2
20 yards

3

15 yards

4

3

Area 1
20 yards

1

2

GK 10 yards

Practice 5 – passing techniques in a conditioned game.

Running, Dribbling and Changing Direction with the Ball

Definition

Being able to move at pace, whilst keeping the ball under control. This is illustrated in the game by players running into space with the ball, dribbling past the opposition or turning in order to create new offensive opportunities.

Why is it Fundamental?

Teams consistently win games when they make good attacking decisions, and positive forward movements with the ball are an important part of any attacking strategy.

Running at the opposition will commit them into a defensive decision; perhaps it will lure them out of position, or set up a 1 v 1 duel. Turning, on the other hand, changes the direction of play, which will allow the team in possession to exploit space away from the ball and find any weaknesses in defensive cover.

Individual Development

As has previously been established, repetition and good practice is the only way for an individual player

to develop technique; the more practice she does, the more familiar she will become with the associated movement patterns. She should be able to move easily with the ball without the need to look at her feet; she will develop an intuitive feeling for it. Then, with familiarity comes confidence, and a confident player will be more prepared to try the technique on the pitch when up against the opposition.

Practice can be undertaken individually with players being encouraged to watch, copy and improvise the skills shown by the world's best players – both male and female. A player with a ball and a few cones is only limited by her enthusiasm and imagination. She can set out different slalom tracks in which to practise moving

Running with the ball course.

Straight-line dribbling slalom course.

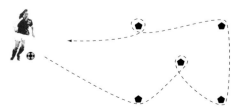

Dribbling and turning slalom course.

England youth international, Remi Allen, demonstrating her dribbling skills.

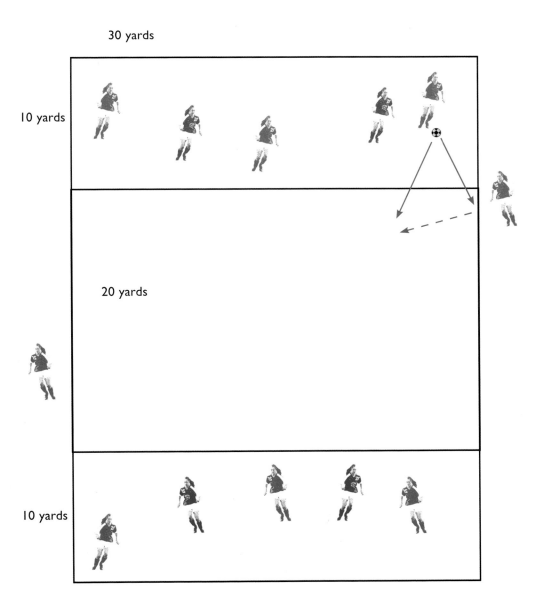

30 yards

10 yards

20 yards

10 yards

Practice 7 – directional running with the ball.

Dribbling

Dribbling relates to a range of techniques that are used by an attacking player to beat and take the ball past a defender. There are many variations on the simple dribbling move involving feints, flicks, fakes and a change of pace. The more complex, eye-catching movements are often given the name of the player who famously first used it, meaning that dribbling is an exciting, as well as a fun technique to coach as well as practise.

When teaching dribbling, the tempo of the practice must be high and players should be urged to be positive, as well as aggressive, with the ball. Confidence is also an important factor and this can be developed through lots of praise and structuring the practice to allow success.

Standard Teaching Points

- Controlled approach. On approach to the defender, the ball should be close and under control, but not under the player's body.
- Awareness. The player's head is up and she should be aware of the defender's position.
- Faking and feinting. The defender is wrong-footed and put off-balance by the player pretending to take the ball in one direction. She makes a fake movement with her foot or dummies with her upper body.
- Accelerate away. The touch on the ball should be executed quickly so that the player can change the direction of her movement and burst away from the defender. Bent knees and a low centre of gravity will allow the player to change her pace.

Arsenal's Helen Lander wrong-footing her opponent.

- Cut off the defender's line of recovery. After beating the defender, the player with the ball cuts into the line of the defender's recovery, making it difficult for her to try to win the ball back.

A controlled approach.

Dummying to wrong-foot the defender.

Accelerating away.

Turning with the Ball

Turning techniques are essentially dribbling moves that allow the player to turn out of trouble, or to change the direction of play. There are many imaginative moves that involve fakes and feints, as well as contact with the ball using all parts of the foot.

* Cutting the ball back with the inside or outside of the foot.
* Stopping the ball with the sole of the foot then dragging it back.
* Back-heeling the ball.
* Stepping over the ball with one foot and using the outside of the other foot to push it back.
* A Cruyff or Ronaldo turn are two of many manoeuvres named after famous players.

When teaching turning the organization for the practice must be realistic and the tempo high. Players should be positive and confident on the ball when trying to turn.

The Cruyff Turn

* The player shapes up as if to shoot or play a long pass by placing her non-kicking foot alongside the ball.
* The kicking foot moves to the front of the ball, turns inwards and pushes it back in the direction that she has come from, using the inside of her foot.
* As she pivots, her next touch on the ball is with the outside of her non-kicking foot and she accelerates away.
* In the photograph to the right the player will use the inside of her right foot to turn back in the direction she came.

The Drag Back

* The player stops any forward movement by placing her foot on top of the ball.
* She drags it back under her body using the sole of her foot and pivoting on her standing foot at the same time.
* After turning, she pushes the ball away from her by using the outside of the foot that dragged the ball back and accelerates away.
* In the photograph overleaf the player is using her left foot to turn.

The Stop Turn

* The player stops the forward motion of the ball by placing her foot on top of it.
* She steps past the ball and plants the same foot on the ground beyond it.

Arsenal's Suzanne Grant turns away from the challenge.

The Cruyff turn.

The drag back.

The stop turn.

- The player pushes the ball back in the direction she came from with the outside of her other foot.
- In the photograph above right the player has stopped the ball with her right foot and is about to push it away with her left foot.

Standard Teaching Points
- Controlled approach. The ball should be close and under control, but not under the player's body.

- Awareness. The player's head is up and she should be aware of the defender's position; if she is on the left, then the ball should be shielded with her body and the right foot used to turn away. Conversely, if the defender is on the right, then the left foot should be used to turn.
- Contact on the ball. The player should remain balanced and execute the technique quickly.
- Accelerate away. Bent knees and a low centre of gravity will allow the player to change her direction efficiently and burst away from the defender.

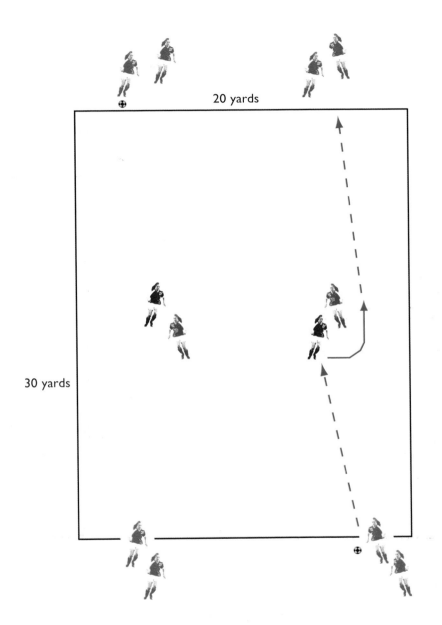

20 yards

30 yards

Practice 10 – turning skill.

Practice 11

Skill level – intermediates.

Purpose
To develop dribbling and turning skills in a competitive environment.

Number of Players
Whole squad, excluding the goalkeepers.

Size of Area
- Overall size: 40 × 30 yards.
- End-zone size: 15 × 30 yards.
- Middle-zone size: 10 × 30 yards.

Type of Session
A skills-development practice that is suitable for players of all ages.

Timing
20 minutes.

Organization
- Players are split into four groups:
  - Two groups work on the outside of each end zone.
  - One group is in the middle zone.
  - One group has a ball each.
- The players with the ball pass to any player at the end zone; they move to make a good receiving angle and receive the return. They turn towards the opposite end zone and dribble at the players in the middle area in order to practise their dribbling techniques. After they have beaten a player in the middle zone, they pass to the opposite end zone and the practice begins again.

- The players in the middle zone are conditioned only to move one step in either direction in an attempt to win the ball.
- Players are given the responsibility to exchange roles. For example, when receiving a pass, an end-zone player could decide to run the ball into the area instead of returning it. In this case the passing player takes her place. The central players might swap roles when they win a ball.

Teaching Points
General good practice:
- All players should be bright and confident on the ball.
- The quality of the passing and receiving should be high.
- The tempo of the practice should be realistic.
- Players must concentrate.

The skill of turning:
- Create space.
- Quality of pass.
- Turning technique.
- End product.

The skill of dribbling:
- Controlled and confident.
- Awareness.
- Fake, feint and dummy.
- Change of pace and accelerate away.
- End product.

Suggested Progressions and Challenges
- Challenge the players to find different ways of turning, perhaps specifying a no-touch turn or a one-touch turn and so on.
- The defenders are initially passive but should apply progressively more pressure as the practice progresses.

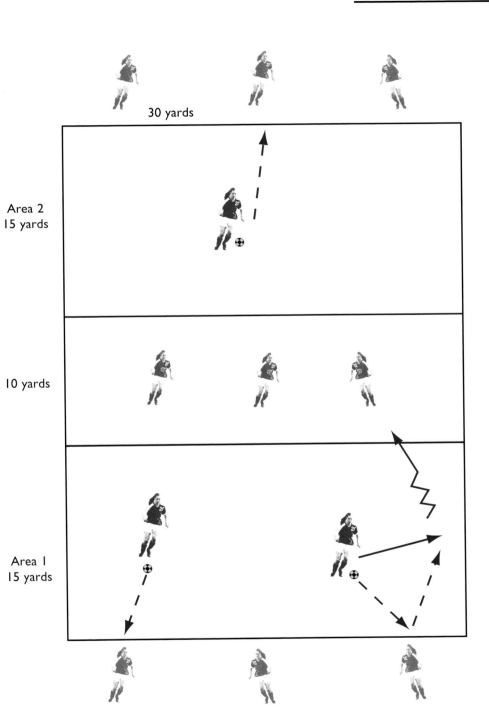

Practice 11 – dribbling and turning skills.

Practice 12

Skill level – intermediates.

Purpose
To develop dribbling and turning skills in a small game.

Number of Players
Whole squad, excluding the goalkeepers.

Size of Area
- Overall size: 40 × 30 yards.
- End-zone size: 15 × 30 yards.
- Middle-zone size 10 × 30 yards.

Type of Session
A skills-development practice that can be a simple progression from Practice 11.

Timing
20 minutes.

Organization
- The players are split into two equal teams of six players, with four players working in one end zone and two in the other end zone.
- The aim of the game is to dribble the ball over the opposite end line. The team in possession of the ball work it forward by.
  - passing it to their team-mates in the other end zone
    or
  - dribbling it from the zone they are in through the middle zone.
- Players must stay inside their own zone unless:
  - They dribble the ball into the middle zone.
  - The player about to receive a forward pass across the end zones can move unchallenged into the middle zone to control the ball.
  - As the ball is passed forward, a third player can move through the middle to support, as illustrated opposite.

- In all cases, the player moving forward through the middle zone can stay until the move breaks down and the other team has the ball.
- When possession is lost or the end line is reached the successful team must first regain its shape before they can try to win the ball back from the opposition; in other words, four players in one end zone and two players in the other.

Teaching Points
General good practice:
- All players should be bright and confident on the ball.
- The tempo of the practice should be realistic.
- Players should be positive, with the coach urging them to try out their dribbling and turning techniques at every opportunity.
- Players must concentrate.

The skill of dribbling:
- Awareness of space.
- Controlled and confident.
- Dribbling technique.
- Cut off the line of recovery.
- End product.

The skill of turning:
- Awareness of space.
- Create space.
- Quality of pass.
- Turning technique.
- End product.

Suggested Progressions and Challenges
- Award a point for each time a player attempts to turn or dribble against an opponent.
- Make play totally free, defending players are allowed in the middle zone.
- Include a goal and goalkeepers so that each team has a realistic target to attack and defend rather than just a line.

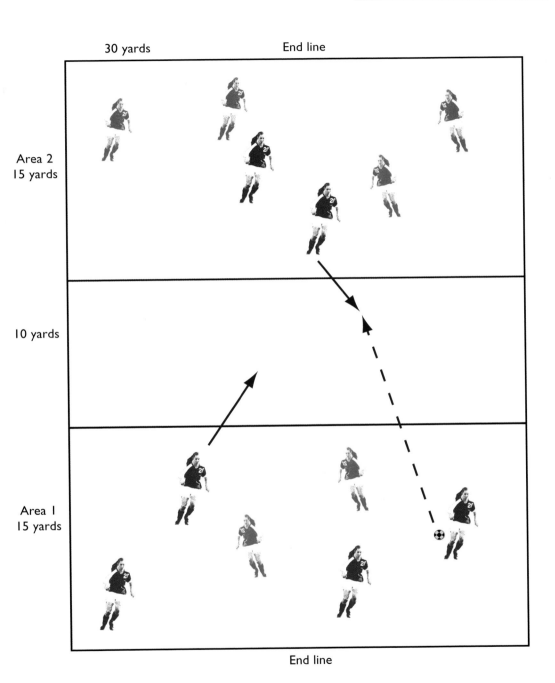

30 yards

End line

Area 2
15 yards

10 yards

Area 1
15 yards

End line

Practice 12 – dribbling and turning skills in a small-game environment.

Heading

Definition
Contact with an aerial ball by the forehead.

Why is it Fundamental?
Heading is a skill unique to football, and having the confidence to be first to the ball in an aerial challenge can make the difference between winning or losing games. A proportion of any football match is played in the air, as well as on the ground. Long, forward passes, diagonal balls and crosses all have the potential to create situations that demand headers by players from either team.

It should be noted that defensive heading techniques and attacking heading techniques are slightly different. Defensive headers require distance and height in order to clear a ball safely, whereas attacking headers require more finesse. They could be directed at goal, down towards the ground, cushioned for control, a glancing header or a flick-on. The situation may require the attacker to dive into the path of the ball or to challenge the defender or goalkeeper. Each type of header requires a slightly different approach to the ball, as well as a slightly different point of contact on the ball.

Heading is an intimidating technique to teach, particularly to young and inexperienced players. There is an obvious fear of being hurt by the ball, as well as a reluctance to challenge another player for an aerial ball.

Individual Development

When working to develop heading the coach must adopt a step-by-step approach in order to build confidence and create conditions which allow the player to be successful. In this way good technique will be learnt in a safe environment.

It is important to challenge players but they should not be pushed too quickly as the confidence that has been built up to head the ball can easily be destroyed by one mis-timed, badly contacted header.

Practice should be frequent but only for short periods of time and the use of the forehead only as the contact point on the ball repeatedly emphasized. Practices must only progress at a pace that each player is comfortable with. Softer balls can also be used.

Standard Teaching Points
- Stance. The player starts in a balanced, semi-crouched position, either square on to the ball or sideways-on to the ball. The crouch and strong back will allow the upper body to act as a 'pivot' in order to propel the head forward for the forehead to make contact on the ball.
- Timing. The player should assess the flight of the ball, timing the jump or the upper-body movement to meet and attack the ball, rather than waiting for it to hit the head.
- Contact. The eyes should remain open and 'watch the ball on to the forehead'. Contact is through the middle of the back of the ball. To head high and long, the contact should be on the lower half of the ball and to head low and down, the contact should be just over the horizontal mid point.
- Using the body. A combination of starting from a balanced position and good timing to attack the ball will ensure that the body is balanced when contact is made. Arms should be out to aid balance and the upper body should be used to propel the forehead through the ball. Arching the back and then attacking the ball will impart pace and power.

Teaching the Correct Contact on the Ball
- The player stands in a balanced position with her legs shoulder-distance apart and knees slightly bent.
- She holds the ball in front of her, just above the eye line. It should be a comfortable, bent-arm distance away from the face.

Faye White wins an aerial battle following an England corner.

Juggling to Develop Confidence

Attempting to keep the ball in the air, either individually or with a partner.

Challenging a Partner

- Players should work about 10 yards apart with one ball.
- The ball is served just above the receiver's head, to develop timing and to encourage her to jump to head the ball.
- The receiver could start with her back to the server. She turns on the command of the server, locates the ball and heads it back.

Working in Threes

- Player one throws to player two, who heads the ball for player three to control or catch. Player three throws to player one and so on. Players new to directional heading would be static in order to encourage good technique, but, as they become confident, they can move within a small area. This will force the heading player to scan for her target and then adjust her feet and body position to ensure that the ball reaches the target player.
- One player serves and one player receives. The third player acts as a defender who is located as an obstruction in front of the receiver. The ball is thrown above the defensive player's head for the receiver to jump, head and return. As confidence develops, the throw would be placed lower so that it is barely above the defender's head when the target player makes contact with the ball.

Balanced, watching the ball.

- Holding the ball still, she arches her back and moves her head forward to make contact with the ball.
- The ball is 'punched' out of her hands towards a partner or a wall.

Timing the movement to meet the ball.

Eyes open, watching the ball.

Using the body to impart pace and power.

Group Development

Practice 13

Skill level – beginners.

Purpose
To practise defensive heading techniques.

Number of Players
Whole squad, excluding the goalkeepers.

Size of Area
- Overall size: 40 × 30 yards.
- Central-zone size: 20 × 10 yards.

Type of Session
Unopposed technical heading practice.

Timing
15 minutes, with the time that each group spends heading the ball being carefully monitored.

Organization
- Players are split into two groups. The players who will be heading the ball work inside the central zone and the servers are spread around the edge of the outer area.
- Each server has a ball and throws it into the central area using a throw-in technique.
- The players in the central area must head the ball back towards the server, attempting to head it high and over their head.
- Once they have headed the ball, the receiver moves off to find another server.
- The groups rotate roles after a short period of time.

Teaching Points
General good practice:
- The session should be conducted at a lively pace.
- Insist on a legal throw-in.
- There should be verbal communication and eye contact between the server and the receiver.

Defending headers:
- Move into line with the ball facing square-on to the target.
- Balanced stance with knees bent ready to attack the ball.
- Timing to jump and meet the ball. A strong back and a straight body will help to provide distance.
- Contact through the lower middle of the back of the ball helps to provide height.
- Follow-through and a balanced landing leaving the player ready to move on to the next server.

Suggested Challenges and Progressions
Add a challenging player or players into the central zone. Initially they can only provide passive pressure to the receivers, though eventually they should be allowed to move and fully challenge for the ball.

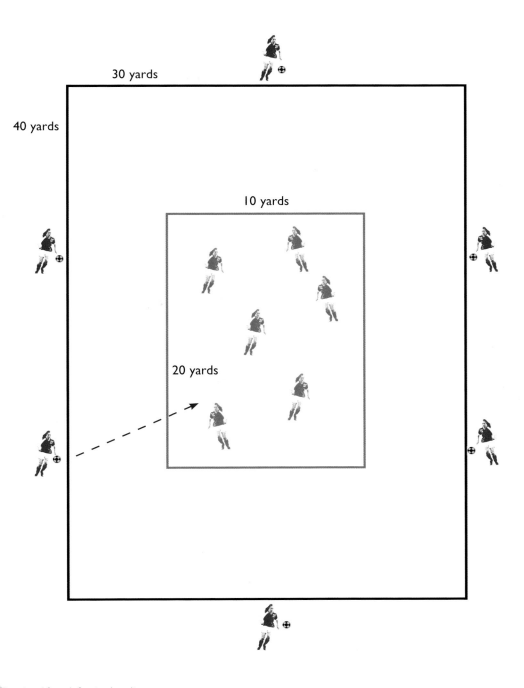

30 yards

40 yards

10 yards

20 yards

Practice 13 – defensive heading.

Practice 14

Skill level – beginners.

Purpose
To practise defending- and attacking-heading techniques.

Number of Players
Whole squad, excluding the goalkeepers.

Size of Area
- Overall size: 25 × 20 yards.
- Central-zone size: 5 × 20 yards.
- End-zone size: 10 × 20 yards.

Type of Session
An unopposed technical-development practice.

Timing
15 minutes.

Organization
- The players are split into three groups and located in each of the three marked zones.
- Players in one end zone have a ball each and use a legal throw-in technique to throw the ball across the middle zone for the players in the opposite end zone to head.
- The practice can be set up for defending headers or attacking headers:
  - Defending headers: the ball will be headed back over the players located in the middle zone.
  - Attacking headers: the players in the middle will sit and the ball has to be headed down to hit them.

Teaching Points
General good practice:
- Insist on a legal throw-in.
- There should be verbal communication and eye contact between the server and the receiver.

Defending headers:
- Move into line with the ball facing square-on to the target.
- Balanced stance with knees bent ready to attack the ball.
- Timing to jump and meet the ball. A strong back and a straight body will help to provide distance.
- Contact through the lower middle of the back of the ball helps to provide height.
- Follow-through and a balanced landing.

Attacking headers:
- Move into line with the ball. Balanced and sideways-on.
- Attack the ball, keeping the eyes open.
- Contact through the upper middle of the back of the ball helps to head the ball down.

Suggested Progressions and Challenges
The conditions on the players in the centre are lifted:
- They can move around within the marked middle zone to make them harder to hit with the ball.
- They can intercept the defensive headers.

20 yards

10 yards

5 yards

10 yards

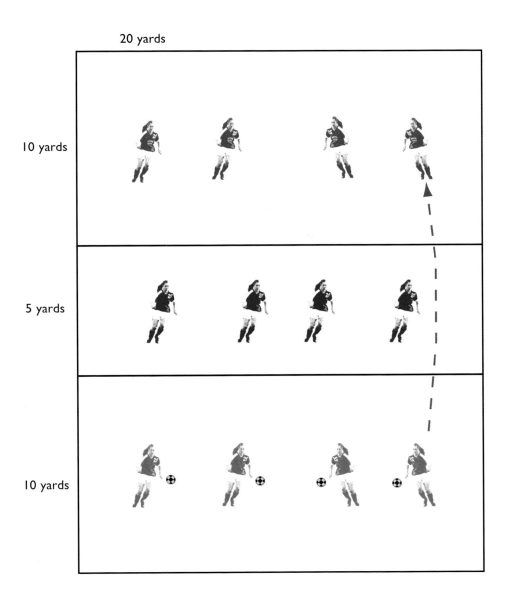

Practice 14 – defensive and attacking heading techniques.

Practice 15

Skill level – beginners, intermediates.

Purpose
To practise heading techniques in a simulated game.

Number of Players
Whole squad, excluding the goalkeepers.

Size of Area
- Overall area size: 20 × 30 yards.

Type of Session
A skills-development practice.

Timing
15 minutes.

Organization
- The players are split into two teams. Each team has a ball.
- One member of the team is responsible for starting play from the back line. She throws the ball to a team-mate, who heads it towards another team-mate for her to catch. Then the sequence begins again.
- The aim of the game is to work the ball from one end line to the other.
- The team is successful when the move finishes with a throw–head–catch sequence on the opposite end line.
- The practice is unopposed, with both teams working in opposite directions at the same time.

Teaching Points
General good practice:
- There should be verbal communication and eye contact between all team members.
- The session should be of a high quality and at a lively pace.

Heading techniques:
- Balance.
- Timing.
- Contact.

Suggested Progressions and Challenges
- The game becomes opposed with a goal and goal-keepers at either end. The ball still moves in the throw–head–catch sequence. If it goes to ground or is intercepted, then possession changes to the other team.
- No physical challenges are initially allowed, this can be introduced towards the end of the practice or with more advanced players.

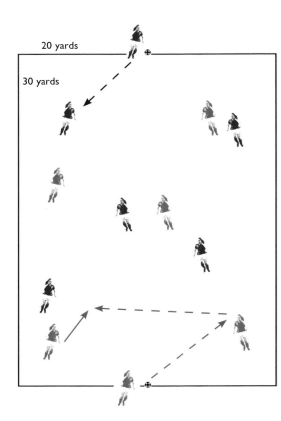

20 yards

30 yards

Practice 15 – throw, head, catch.

Shooting and Finishing

Definition

Shooting is a kicking technique that employs power, pace and direction with the aim of scoring a goal.

Finishing relates to being able to take a goal-scoring opportunity by using any legitimate part of the body to propel the ball towards the goal.

Why is it Fundamental?

Scoring more goals than the other team is the ultimate aim in any football match. Games are won and lost in front of goal, therefore, attacking players have to be able to recognize, as well as take, goal-scoring opportunities. The best goal-scorers are aggressive and confident players with an eye for the opportunity; in other words, they see a chance and take it.

An attacking move should always aim to finish with an attempt on goal.

Developing Shooting

Shooting is as much about selecting the correct kicking technique for the circumstance as it is about technique.

- A driven shot is characterized by pace and power. The player makes contact through the middle of the back of the ball with the laces of the kicking foot.
- The inside of the foot can be used for accurate placement, especially when pace is less important,

to beat the goalkeeper. Note that this is the same technique as used for a push pass.
- A swerving shot can be driven using the inside or outside of the instep.

Finishing is a more general term relating to the player being able to exploit the 'moment'. She might find herself free of the defenders with only the goalkeeper to beat, in which case a chip, a dribble or a well-placed shot could all do the job. The ball may have been crossed low towards goal, in which case a diving header or volley could provide the finishing touch. The opportunity may be a half-chance with a loose ball within scoring range. Here a knee or shin or head could be used to deflect the ball into the goal.

The most important attacking attribute for any successful team must be their attitude towards goal-scoring opportunities and it is the coach's responsibility to create a realistic practice that mimics the intensity of the penalty area during the game. Whenever there is space, and the ball is within goal-scoring range, players should be encouraged to take the chance to score. The attacking third is the place to take risks, it's defended the heaviest with both space and time being severely limited. Quick shooting and one-touch finishing are as much an attitude as they are techniques.

Players can be conditioned into a goal-scoring mindset by practising their finishing regularly. Service should be varied, with the ball moving towards the kicker, away from the kicker, across the kicker from the right and the left. It should also be served in the air and on the ground. The areas used for the practice should

England's Katie Chapman takes a difficult shooting opportunity from the edge of the Spanish penalty area.

Ellen White lines up for a shot at goal during an England training session.

The ball is placed rather than driven.

be tight in order to limit the spaces and keep the practice challenging as well as realistic.

Standard Teaching Points

- Observe the goalkeeper. The position of the goal-keeper off the line and between the posts will help the striker make up her mind which part of the goal to shoot at and what technique to use. As always, players should be encouraged to 'play with their head up', to scan as they move with the ball towards the goal.
- Accuracy over power. There is nothing as satis-fying as seeing and hearing the ball hit into the back of the net. However, a spectacular finish is only worth the same as a simple tap in, namely a goal. Therefore players must be composed in front of goal and be prepared to 'pass the ball into the goal'. It is better to keep the ball on-target, as there is always a chance of a deflection, rather than blasting the ball over the bar or wide of the post. Concentration and composure are the most vital attributes for a striker to have in front of goal.
- Balance. As the ball approaches, the player should watch it all the way on to her foot so that her

body is properly balanced over the ball at the moment of contact.
- The placement of the non-kicking foot is important. When it is level with the ball and slightly to the side, the rest of the body will be properly balanced and aligned over the ball.
- Upon the point of contact, the knee is over the ball, the head is steady and the eyes are looking at the ball.
- Good balance ensures the leg gets a full swing at the ball and is able to follow-through, transferring the momentum of the body completely into the kick.
- Contact on the ball. Contact should be made through the middle or top-half of the back of the ball in order to keep it low. Balls at chest height are easier for the goalkeeper to gather than balls placed low into the corners of the goal. The ball can be driven straight using the laces (instep) or with a small amount of swerve imparted by using the front part of the instep and either slightly inside or outside, depending upon the direction that the player requires the swerve. It can also be taken on the volley or half-volley, as illustrated by the images opposite.

The player is firmly concentrating on the ball, her eyes are firmly fixed on it and she is balanced. Her right ankle is locked, ready to make contact on the ball.

Following a good contact on the ball, the player remains balanced and is able to impart the full force of her body into the shot by following through with her kicking leg.

Group Development

Practice 16

Skill level – beginners, intermediates.

Purpose
To practise one- and two-touch shooting techniques.

Number of Players
Whole squad, can also include the goalkeepers.

Size of Area
- Overall size: 30 × 30 yards, with two full-sized goals at either end line.

Type of Session
An unopposed technical-development practice.

Timing
20 minutes.

Organization
- The players are split equally either side of each goal on each end line. There are two feeders located in the middle of the marked area.
- One player at each end line has a ball. Note that these players should be diagonally opposite each other to allow two players to work safely at the same time.
- The ball is passed in to the feeders, who receive and lay the ball off. The feeder should take no more than two touches.
- The player who passed the ball, follows the pass, looks for the lay-off and shoots at the opposite goal.
- The feeder spins towards this goal ready to finish from any rebounds. After the move has ended,

she joins the players on the end line and the striker stays in the middle to become the next feeder.
- The move starts again from the opposite end line and the sequence is repeated in the other direction.
- There are two balls in play at any one time.

Teaching Points
General good practice:
- Players should keep their shots on-target.
- The session should have a lively pace.

Shooting techniques:
- Observe the position of the goalkeeper.
- Adjust to the position of the ball.
- Composure.
- Contact.
- Finish the rebounds.

Suggested Progression and Challenges
- The feeder should vary the service, even picking the ball up and serving, if necessary, in order to create the correct conditions for volleys and half-volleys.
- The ball should also be laid off at a variety of speeds and angles to challenge the striker.
- The feeder is given the option, when she receives the ball, to turn and shoot, or play the lay-off as before.
- Another player from the same end line chases the striker and tries to prevent the shot.
- A player from the opposite end line moves into the marked area to defend against the striker.
- Vary the type of lay-off by introducing simple movement patterns between the striker and the feeder.
- For example, see figures opposite.

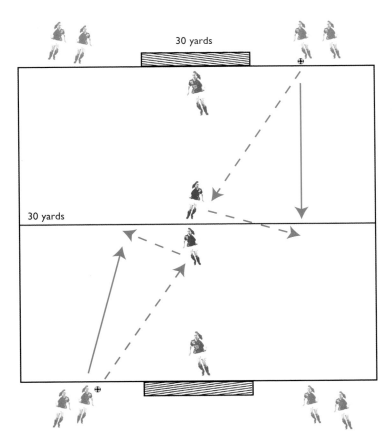

30 yards

30 yards

Practice 16 – one- and two-touch shooting techniques.

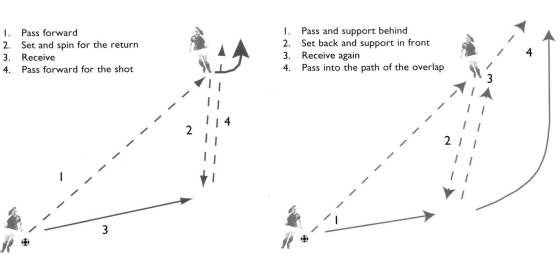

1. Pass forward
2. Set and spin for the return
3. Receive
4. Pass forward for the shot

1. Pass and support behind
2. Set back and support in front
3. Receive again
4. Pass into the path of the overlap

Simple set and spin.

Simple set and overlap.

Practice 17

Skill level – beginners, intermediates.

Purpose
To practise shooting and finishing skills.

Number of Players
Whole squad, can also include the goalkeepers.

Size of Area
Overall size: 30 × 30 yards, with two full-sized goals at either end line.

Type of Session
A skills-development practice.

Timing
20 minutes.

Organization
*   The players are organized into two equal teams, each with a goalkeeper.
*   The goalkeeper starts with the ball and rolls it out, either to her left or right.
*   The first two players, one from either side of the goal, move into the playing area with an aim to take a shot at goal as quickly as possible.
*   One player from the opposite end line moves into the playing area to act as a defender; if she wins the ball, she can attack the other goal.
*   After the shot and any rebounds, all three players take their place at the back of the opposite end line.
*   Play then re-starts from the other end.

Teaching Points
General good practice:
*   Players should take every opportunity to shoot at goal.
*   Shots should be on-target.
*   The session should have a lively pace.

Shooting and finishing techniques:
*   Observe the position of the goalkeeper.
*   Adjust to the position of the ball.
*   Composure.
*   Contact.
*   Finish the rebounds.

Suggested Progression
The game progresses into a 2 v 2 with a second defender moving into the player area from the defending end line.

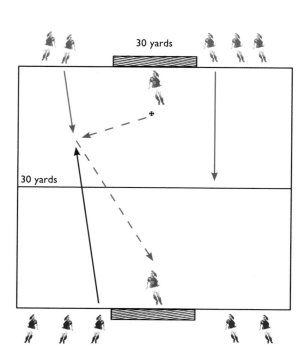

30 yards

30 yards

Practice 17 – shooting and finishing skills.

Practice 18

Skill level – intermediates.

Purpose
To practise shooting and finishing skills.

Number of Players
Whole squad, including the goalkeepers.

Size of Area
Overall size: 30 × 30 yards, with two full-sized goals at either end line.

Type of Session
A skills-development practice in a realistic small-sided game environment.

Timing
30 minutes.

Organization
The players are organized into three equal teams and there is a goalkeeper in each goal.
Two teams play within the marked area in a 4 v 4 small-sided game. The other team spreads out on either sideline to act as feeders, if the ball goes out of play. They should be ready to move on to the playing area once a goal is scored.
The goalkeeper starts with the ball and rolls it out to a member of her team. The size of the playing area means that the team in possession should take every opportunity to shoot at the opposition goal.

- When a goal is scored, the team that conceded the goal comes off the playing area. The team on the sideline comes into the playing area and defends the vacant goal.
- Play restarts from the goalkeeper who has conceded the goal, serving to the team who has just come on to the playing area.

Teaching Points
General good practice:
- Players should take every opportunity to shoot at goal.
- Shots should be on-target.
- The session should have a lively pace.

Shooting and finishing techniques:
- Observe the position of the goalkeeper.
- Adjust to the position of the ball.
- Composure.
- Contact.
- Finish the rebounds.

Suggested Progression
- The team on the sidelines can only feed an aerial ball or a cross for a volley or a header.
- Goals can only be scored from a cross.

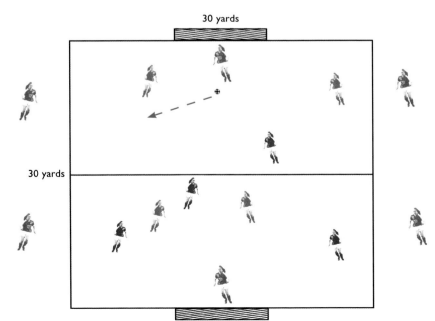

30 yards

30 yards

Practice 18 – finishing skills.

CHAPTER 6

PRINCIPLES OF DEFENCE

Definition

Defending is the ability of the team, and the individual, to prevent the opposition from scoring a goal. Good defending will restrict forward play and win the ball back, either in the 1 v 1 or by forcing an error.

Why is it Fundamental?

If attacking play can be said to be an art, then defending is very much a science, where angles, distances and decision-making are as important as individual technique. Players must understand where and how to position themselves in order to restrict the opposition team's attacking opportunities. The principles of a good defence are:

Pressure. If the player with the ball is put under pressure, her time and space to decide what to do with it is severely restricted.

Cover. A defender who pressurizes the player with the ball needs to be supported, so that if she is beaten there is a second defender available to apply pressure. Good cover also restricts opportunities for playing the ball forward.

Balance and compactness. A team that is balanced and compact will limit the opportunities for forward play and be able to defend the vulnerable and key areas of the pitch, thereby restricting the chances for penetrating attacking moves from the opposition.

Individually aggressive and committed defending, coupled with patience and self-discipline, is the foundation of a strong team defence, and players should be taught to read the situation carefully before reacting. Defending, therefore, is primarily about decisions:

- Should she press the player with the ball or fill the space and hold her position?
- Should she tackle to try to win the ball or jockey to buy time for her team?
- Which side should she mark her immediate opponent and how close should she be?
- Should she track the runner and if so how far?

Good decision-making should also be supported by sound individual defending techniques, which all players should be taught, regardless of their playing position. This involves learning how to slow or stop the momentum of the attack by pressing their immediate opponent in a 1 v 1.

LEFT: Tracking a Spanish defender.

RIGHT: Strong and committed defending.

Defending as an Individual

Applying Pressure to an Opponent

The aim of the individual defender is to keep the ball and the player in front of her. Her objectives will vary with each different situation:

- If the ball can be intercepted or won before the opponent has time to secure it, then the defender should move in quickly with a committed and strong challenge.
- If the opponent has secured the ball, then the defender's aim is to make play predictable by forcing it in one direction and restricting opportunities for forward play.
- If the opponent has her back to the defender, then the turn should be prevented and play forced backwards.
- Patient defending will delay the opposition, giving time for the rest of the team to recover into a good defensive shape.
- Clever defending recognizes the moment to challenge for the ball. The tackle should be made from a balanced position with confidence and aggression.

Standard Teaching Points

Travel as the Ball Travels

- The defender moves quickly as the ball is moving in order to deny time and space to her immediate (nearest) opponent.
- As she moves, the defender watches the ball as well as her opponent. She should be ready to adopt a defensive stance as soon as contact is made with the ball.
- The defender should challenge and win the ball if her opponent has no opportunity to bring it under control, or fails to secure it with her first touch.
- The approach can be either the quickest route to the ball or a curved run, depending upon the circumstances.
  - The quickest route should be taken if the defender thinks she can win the ball or if her opponent has her back to play.
  - A curved run would be more appropriate where the opponent is to be forced in one direction.

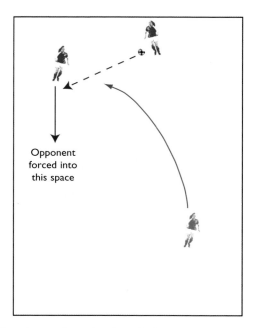

Curved run to force play down the line.

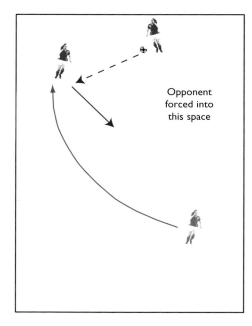

Curved run to force play inside.

Watching the ball and stopping the turn.

Getting too tight.

Defensive Stance

- The defender should adopt a balanced stance on the balls of her feet. Her head is steady watching the ball.
- Ideally, she should be about an arm's length away from her opponent. If she is positioned too close:
     A player who is 'faced up' will be able to push the ball past her.
     An opponent who has her back turned could 'roll' her, shielding the ball as she turns.
- Conversely a defender who is too far away from her opponent will have no effect and be unable to exert any useful pressure.
- The stance should be sideways in order to retain mobility and make play predictable.

In diagram a (right), the defender is inviting her opponent to play into the space shown by the arrow. This could be towards the touchline, on to the opponent's weaker foot or towards an area that is well-defended by the rest of the team.

In diagram b (right), the defender is square-on to her opponent and, therefore, unsure whether the ball will be pushed to the right or the left. Consequently her reaction and recovery will be slow giving the initiative to the attacker.

(a)

Making play predictable.

(b)

Giving the initiative to the attacking player.

Patience, Delay and Jockeying

- By adopting a good defensive stance, the defender is beginning to gain the initiative and she should now be prepared to watch, wait and select the correct moment to challenge for the ball.
- Her footwork is important and she should move in relation to the movement of the ball, maintaining her distance as well as 'jockeying' her opponent in a predictable direction.
- She should take small, shuffling steps to remain balanced at all times. When there is a change of direction, her sideways stance is maintained by pivoting from the hips – a movement that will prevent her legs from becoming crossed.
- Defenders should be patient enough to wait for the right moment to win the ball, slowing the momentum of the attack and then forcing the opponent to play sideways or backwards. This can be a better option than winning the ball in some circumstances.

Tackling

- The defender should aim to stay on her feet, watching the ball carefully, until the moment to tackle presents itself. Opportunities to win the ball come from:

    Hesitation by the attacking player.
    Mis-control by the attacking player.
    An attempt by the attacking player to turn.
    The defender faking to tackle to gain the initiative in the confrontation.

- Tackles should be made confidently from a balanced position, in order to give strength to the challenge. The defender should normally stay on her feet but there are occasions when she will need to go to ground or make a sliding tackle.
- The defender can tackle with the front or the back foot:

    When tackling with the front foot, the defender leans in towards the ball and pokes it away.
    Tackling off the back foot has the full force and balance of the body behind it. The defender steps into the ball and, with a strong, locked ankle, challenges with a block tackle using the inside of her foot.

- Once the decision is made to tackle, it should be followed through without hesitation, as this can put a player off-balance and, in some unfortunate circumstances, lead to injury.

Tackling off the front foot.

Practice 19

Skill level – all abilities.

Purpose
To teach, develop and reinforce the technique of defensive footwork.

Number of Players
Whole squad, excluding goalkeepers.

Size of Area
Players work individually and in pairs over a maximum distance of 20 yards.

Type of Session
An introductory footwork-development exercise, which could be used as a short warm-up activity or as an introduction to a specific defending practice.

Timing
10 minutes.

Organization
- The squad is organized in a small area, as shown by the diagram below. Each player has a ball placed about 15 yards in front of them.

- On the signal, they make a pressurizing run towards the ball, coming to a stop at the correct distance and with the correct stance.
- Their run and positioning should be in a slight curve, to show that they understand how to force play in one direction.
- The first simple exercise can be progressed by pairing the players up with a ball between two. One player is designated as the defender.
- They are about 10 yards apart and play a short series of one-touch passes. On the signal, the designated defender passes the ball, then runs to press.
- As the ball is controlled, the defender takes up a good, defensive stance. They work slowly in a 'zig-zag' in the direction shown (see diagram below) for a distance of 15 to 20 yards.
- The defending should be passive with the emphasis on the quality of the defenders' footwork.

Teaching Points
- Speed of approach.
- Angle of approach with a curved run.
- Distance from the ball and maintaining the distance from the ball.
- Sideways stance and maintaining a sideways stance.

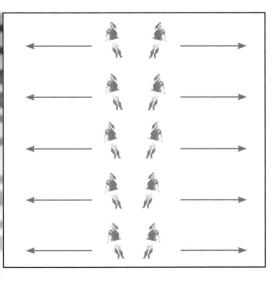

Practice 19 – defending footwork exercises, # 1.

Practice 19 – defending footwork exercises, # 2.

Practice 20

Skill level – all abilities.

Purpose
To teach, develop and reinforce pressurizing techniques.

Number of Players
Whole squad, excluding goalkeepers.

Size of Area
Each area sized 20 × 10 yards.

Type of Session
Technical-development practice.

Timing
15 minutes.

Organization
- The squad is divided into a number of small groups. Each group has its own marked area and is split into two smaller groups. Each is located on the corner of the marked area, diagonally opposite the other.
- The first two players play a short sequence of passes to create a moving ball.

- The defender passes the ball to the attacker and follows the pass, in order to press.
- The attacker receives the ball and attacks the marked target by trying to dribble the ball through it.
- If the defender wins the ball she should turn defence into attack by attempting to dribble it over the line behind the attacker.
- When the ball goes out or one player scores, the next pair move on to the area.

Teaching Points
- Travel as the ball travels.
- Angle of approach with a curved run to block off the direct route to the target and force play away from it.
- Defensive footwork.
- Winning the ball through a tackle or remaining patient and forcing play off the pitch.

Progression – to Stop the Turn
- This practice can be adapted to teach the defender how to stop an attacker from turning.
- One attacker is located in the centre of the area facing away from the defender. She receives a pass from a team-mate and attempts to turn and then dribble the ball through the shaded target. Play continues as before.

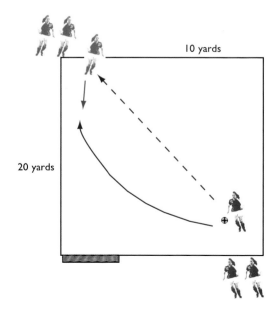

Practice 20 – pressurizing in a 1 v 1.

Practice 21

Skill level – all abilities.

Purpose
To teach, develop and reinforce the importance of pressurizing the player with the ball.

Number of Players
Whole squad, excluding goalkeepers.

Size of Area
- 20 × 30 yards.

Type of Session
A skills-development practice on a small-game environment.

Timing
15 minutes.

Organization
- Twelve players are organized into three teams of four. One team is positioned inside the playing area, with the other two beginning the practice outside the area.
- The ball is played by the coach to the team located inside the marked area. Their aim is to keep possession for as long as possible. One team from outside the marked area moves into the area as the ball travels and attempts to win it. The other team rests.
- When the defending team win the ball, the other team leaves the marked area and the resting team takes their place.

Teaching Points
- The first defender, i.e. the player who is nearest to the ball, must press and try to create the 1 v 1.
- Travel as the ball travels.
- Angle of approach with a curved run to force play towards team-mates, or a direct run to stop the turn.
- Defensive footwork.
- Winning the ball through a tackle or remaining patient and making the pass difficult.

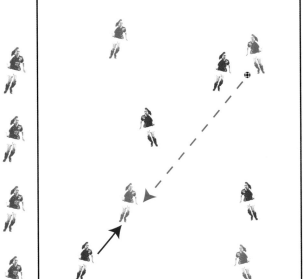

20 yards

30 yards

Practice 21 – creating the 1 v 1.

Practice 22

Skill level – all abilities.

Purpose

To reinforce the importance of pressurizing the player with the ball and to introduce the concept of cover.

Number of Players

Whole squad, excluding goalkeepers.

Size of Area

*   40 × 30 yards.
*   Corner target zone: 10 × 10 yards.

Type of Session

A skills-development practice in a small-sided game environment.

Timing

20 minutes.

Organization

*   Twelve players are organized into two teams of five with two target players who are located in the corner target areas.
*   The teams play against each other with an aim to get the ball to either one of the target players.
*   When a target player receives the ball, she feeds it back to the other team and the practice begins again.

Teaching Points

*   First defender – press the ball:
    *   Travel as the ball travels.
    *   Angle of approach.
    *   Defensive footwork.
    *   Winning the ball through a tackle or remaining patient and making the pass difficult.
*   Team compactness and cover.

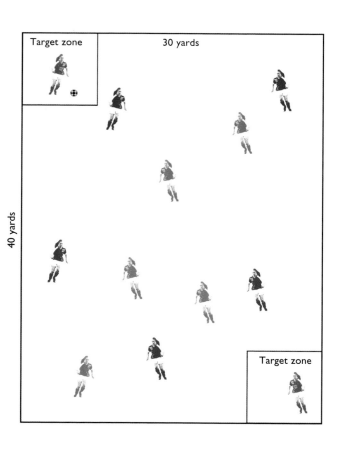

Practice 22 – pressurizing in a small-sided game.

CHAPTER 7

PRINCIPLES OF ATTACK

Good attacking skills are the key to winning games and fundamental to success in attack is a team's ability to create and exploit space. If the principles of team defence are to restrict the spaces by adopting a tight, compact shape, then the principles for team attack should be to break this up, by stretching the defenders and destroying their carefully placed cover.

Make the Pitch Big

The first step for the team that has the ball is to spread out:

* As wide as possible.
* As long as possible.
* Quickly.

By spreading out, the attacking team essentially makes the pitch big. This provides both time and space for that team to be able to establish its attacking moves.

Penetrate

This doesn't mean that every ball should be a forward ball, but it does mean that teams should look to play the ball behind even just one member of the opposition, in order to break down cover, pull players out of position and create opportunities to score goals.

Movement

Movement on and off the ball is the final ingredient for an effective attack. Aggressive forward movement with the ball will commit the opposition defenders into a decision luring them towards the ball and out of position. Away from the ball, defenders can be forced to adjust their position by attacking runs that are made either up and down the pitch, or in diagonals across the front of, or in behind, the unit.

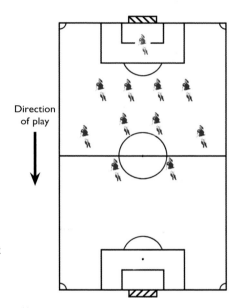

Direction of play

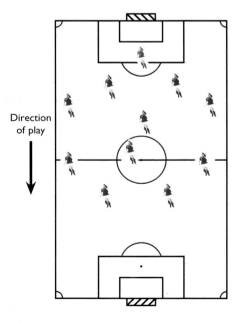

Direction of play

LEFT: It's a goal. Leicester take the lead against Preston.

RIGHT ABOVE: The team in a compact defensive shape.

RIGHT BELOW: Making the pitch big in attack.

Jess Clarke of England in space on the edge of the box reaches to control a long, forward ball.

Creating Space as an Individual

When a team is on the attack, there are a number of decisions that have to be made in order to create opportunities in front of the goal. Typically these are based on:

* The team strategy.
* The momentum of the game.
* Where the ball is now.
* Where the ball should end up.
* The positioning of the opposition.
* The positioning of team-mates.

In order to assist these decisions, individual players need to understand how to create space in preparation for receiving the ball. A supporting player can make the game easier by being available to receive a pass at the correct time, the correct angle and the correct distance away from the player who is passing the ball.

Supporting players should aim to be in an 'open' position, so that they can see the ball as well as the pitch. Upon receiving the ball, her stance will allow her to take her first touch forwards rather than backwards.

Movement into a space should be made quickly and involve short, darting runs that are at angles, either across the front of defenders or behind them. This

makes it difficult for the defender to concentrate on the ball as well as track and react to the runner.

Timing, too, is important and runs can be early to drag defenders out of position or late to catch them by surprise.

Typical Movements to Create Space and Destroy Cover

Checking-Off

* Attacking player A2 makes a movement behind the back shoulder of the defender D2. The defender is forced to adjust her position and loses track of the position of the ball.
* A2 darts across the front of the defender to receive a pass to feet from A1.
* She should try to receive the ball in an open position, so that she is faced up and can attack the defender D2.

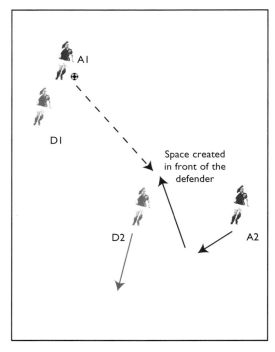

Checking-off. Going long to come short.

* Attacking player A2 makes a movement down the line and back towards her own goal.
* If the defender D2 adjusts her position to track the movement, A2 will spin and look for a long ball to be played into her path and behind D2.

If the defender D2 stays where she is, the ball will be passed to the feet of A2 for her to face up and attack defender D2.

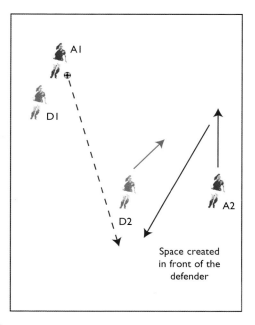

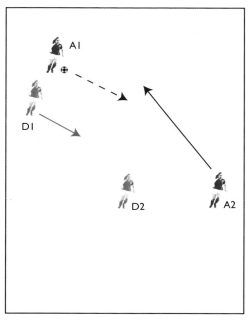

The take-over.

Checking-off. Coming short to go long.

- Turn in-field and attempt to beat the defender D2.
- Set the ball back to a third player for her to pass a long, forward ball into the path of A1.

Take-Overs

Attacking player A1 dribbles the ball across the pitch towards A2.

Attacking player A2 moves towards A1, passing her on the side furthest away from the defender. The defender D1 adjusts her position to track the movement of A1 and defender D2 adjusts her position to track the run of A2.

Space is created down either side of the defenders as they are brought together by the movement of both attackers.

Either A2 can take the ball from A1 and continue the run in-field with the ball, or they can dummy the take-over and A1 continues her movement down the line.

Over-Laps

Attacking player A2 steps across the front of defender D2 and receives a pass from A1.

A1 follows the pass around the outside of A2 and continues the run down the line.

A2 can do one of the following:
- Pass the ball into the path of the oncoming A1 for her to carry the ball down the line.

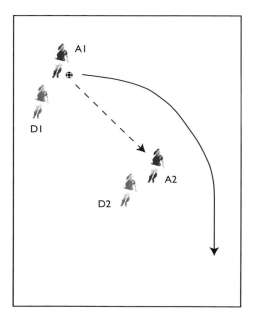

The overlapping run.

CHAPTER 8

GOALKEEPING

The goalkeeper is unique within the team: she is the last line of defence or the first line of attack and, more often than not, it is her performance that determines the outcome of the game.

Although a goalkeeper can often be unoccupied for large segments of the game, her position on the pitch allows her to see the whole game and she is, therefore, involved in it in a way that is unlike any other member of the team. Rather than let her team-mates rely on her only when she has the ball, the goalkeeper should work hard to impose her presence throughout the entire game, both vocally and positionally, making sure that she both supports, as well as inspires, her team.

Goalkeeping is a specialist position and, being the only player who is able to use her hands, it requires specialist and individual coaching. However, it should be noted that one-to-one coaching often sets the goalkeeper apart and, although it is an excellent environment for individual development, the team coach should ensure that she is involved in, and contributes to, team sessions wherever possible.

Attributes for Successful Goalkeeping

Good goalkeeping is about sound knowledge and understanding of the role, supported by good technique, physical attributes and psychological strength.

Technical/Tactical Attributes

Competence in core techniques:

- Handling.
- Footwork.
- Shot stopping.
- Dealing with crosses and high balls.
- Distribution.

LEFT: Helen Alderson claims the ball.

RIGHT: The view from the goal-line.

Thorough understanding of the team's overall strategies and tactics:

- The goalkeeper's positional role in defence.
- The goalkeeper's role and responsibilities in attack.

Physical Attributes

- Physical presence. A female goalkeeper who is also tall has a great advantage; however, it is also important that she should have presence within her goal, is able to dominate her area and has the knack of being able to appear big and difficult to beat.
- Speed and co-ordination. Well co-ordinated movements contribute to the goalkeeper's overall speed of movement around her goal. She requires agility and balance, as well as good reflexes.

Psychological Attributes

- Concentration and focus. The nature of goalkeeping means that she is often in an isolated position, both at training and during the game. To prevent her becoming detached from the team, she must be able to concentrate, ignore distractions and be able to focus on the task in hand.
- Courageous and decisive. A goalkeeper has to be first to the ball in most of the situations in her

The loneliest of roles.

England goalkeepers, Siobhan Chamberlain and Rachel Brown, warming up.

area, therefore she requires a decisive personality that is supported by the courage to act effectively and quickly.

- Communication skills. A good goalkeeper is also a good communicator. Her position on the pitch, behind the rest of the team, is unique: she can see the whole game spread out in front of her. She should use this to inform her team-mates, to organize them, as well as to support and encourage. When play is in and around the goal area, her communication is vital, providing loud and decisive information to her outfield team-mates. For example, a loud and confident call of 'Keeper' (if she is going to gather the ball) or 'Away' (if she wants the defender to clear the ball), provides all the information required for the team to deal effectively with the situation.
- Commitment. By its nature, the position of a goalkeeper is very individual within the context of the team and at times it can be a lonely role. The goalkeeper, therefore, should be a strong and committed character, with a desire to work hard and an innate ability to remain confident in the face of adversity.

Coaching the Goalkeeper

Where at all possible, a head coach should strive to ensure that the goalkeeper receives high-quality and continuous coaching, in order to develop all aspects of her game. The one-to-one environment is perfect for developing the individual, and the training should be structured to allow the goalkeeper realistic practice in all aspects of her game. She should work in short but intense intervals, with an emphasis on correct practice at all times.

The one-to-one nature of goalkeeper coaching also allows space for self-evaluation. Work with a female goalkeeper lends itself to a co-operative coaching method, where the player is able to have input into her own development.

In a game, the goalkeeper will wear gloves and, therefore, it is advisable that these are worn throughout all coaching sessions. By doing this, the goalkeeper will learn to employ the correct techniques in as realistic a way as possible.

The coaching position should be close to the goalkeeper to allow immediate feedback, as well as ensure that a practice is able to maintain its intensity. When working on shot stopping and crosses, the coaching position should be behind the goalkeeper in the goal, which allows the coach to accurately assess the goalkeeper's positioning in relation to the ball.

The basic techniques are outlined below.

The Starting Position

The goalkeeper should maintain a 'ready' position, no matter where the ball is in relation to her goal. From this she is able to react to the movement of the ball, as each situation demands.

- Head. The head should be steady with her eyes on the ball at all times. It should be tilted forwards to ensure that the goalkeeper's body weight is on the balls of her feet.
- Hands. The elbows are tucked in and the hands are at waist height in a 'ready' position, with the

The starting position.

The 'W' position.

fingers outstretched. The palms can be facing in or out, whichever is most comfortable.

- Feet. The feet should be shoulder-width apart, with the knees slightly bent. Because the goal-keeper's head is tilted and her body weight is slightly forwards, she is ready to move in any direction, as the situation demands.

Basic Handling

The goalkeeper should always be ready to receive the ball. No matter how it is travelling towards her, the primary aim should be to get some part of her body behind it, in order to create a barrier between her and the goal. The first barrier is usually her hands and the second barrier some part of her body. The ball should be watched carefully at all times until it has been drawn in to her body and made completely safe.

The 'W' Position
The hands create a large surface area, the palms are up and the fingers spread, the thumbs should be touching

each other. This position creates the 'W' and provides as strong a barrier behind the ball as possible.

Balls at Ground Level
The long barrier (see page 120):
- The goalkeeper moves into line with the ball.
- Her arms are out in front to create the first barrier and her body is sideways-on to provide a second barrier.
- The foot and the knee create the long barrier across the line of the goal.
- The ball is collected, scooped into the chest and secured.

The scoop (see page 120):
- The goalkeeper moves into line with the ball.
- Her feet are together and her arms are out in front to create two barriers.
- Bending from the hips, her hands reach out in front to take the ball as early as possible.
- The little fingers are together and the palms open.
- The ball is scooped up into the chest and secured.
- As an alternative, there are occasions when the goalkeeper would collapse on to the ball to secure it.

The long barrier.

The scoop.

Securing the ball into the body.

Balls at waist height:
- The goalkeeper moves into line and 'sets' with her head, hands and feet as the ball is kicked.
- She watches the ball into her body, relaxes upon impact, and cups her arms around it to trap it and secure possession.

Balls at chest height:
- The goalkeeper moves into line and 'sets' with her head, hands and feet as the ball is kicked.
- The ball is caught as early as possible using the 'W' position in front of her chest.
- She watches the ball into her hands, relaxes upon contact and secures possession by trapping it into her chest.

Balls at head height:
- The goalkeeper moves into line and 'sets' with her head, hands and feet as the ball is kicked.
- The ball is caught as early as possible using the 'W' position in front of her head. In this case, please note that the second barrier is the goalkeeper's head.
- She watches the ball into her hands, her arms should be bent and relaxed upon contact.
- She secures possession by trapping it into her chest.

alls at head height.

Catching a high ball.

alls above head height:

- The goalkeeper moves into line and 'sets' with her head, hands and feet as the ball is kicked.
- She picks out the flight of the ball and times her jump to take the ball at the highest point.
- As the ball is caught, her arms should be straight and reaching towards it. In this case, please note that there is no second barrier.
- She tilts her head to be able to watch the ball firmly into her hands.
- She secures possession by trapping it into her chest.

ootwork and Movement Around the Goal

he footwork that is used by a goalkeeper to move round her area is crucial; it helps her to maintain her alance, remain open to play and provides a solid foun-ation for all her handling and shot stopping. Her move-ents should be a combination of shuffling and gliding, o that she is able to move quickly in response to the novement of the ball. Her legs should never cross, so hat she is able to stop and set at any point in order to eceive the ball or deal with a shot.

Moving Sideways (see page 122)

- Lead with the leg in the direction of travel.
- The sole of the moving foot should just brush the turf.
- Take little, but quick steps with the legs, never crossing them.
- The head should remain steady, with the eyes watching the ball at all times.
- The hands should be 'ready' at waist height.

Moving Forwards or Backwards

- The sole of the moving foot should just brush the turf.
- Take little, but quick steps.
- The goalkeeper should never turn her back to the ball.
- The head should remain steady with the eyes watching the ball at all times.
- The hands should be 'ready' at waist height.

Running Around Goal

To move more quickly in order to deal with crossed balls and the like, the goalkeeper should employ a sprinting technique. The body should remain open to the ball with the eyes watching it at all times.

Moving sideways from the set position.   *The left foot brushes the turf.*   *The right foot follows the left foot.*

Simple Practices to Improve Handling and Footwork

If the goalkeeper is a novice, the coach should emphasize the following:

- The quality of the footwork and, if necessary, sacrifice speed for good technique.
- The goalkeeper's set position as the ball is played towards her.
- The quality of the first and second barrier as the ball is received.

Goalkeeper practice 1

- A row of footballs are placed in front of the goalkeeper.
- The distance between each ball is just wider than the length of her feet.
- She moves forward through the balls in a slalom or, as a variation, over the balls and planting each foot in the space between the balls.
- As she moves she holds a ball steady out in front of her, whilst maintaining good hand placement.

Goalkeeper practice 2

- Marker discs are laid out in a slalom, in front of the goalkeeper.
- The distance between each disc is large enough to allow both feet to be planted next to each other on the turf.
- She moves sideways through the slalom.
- As she moves, the coach will call out 'set', meaning that the goalkeeper will have to stop and assume her set position.

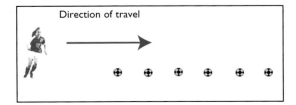

Goalkeeper practice 1 – moving forwards.

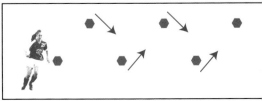

Goalkeeper practice 2 – moving sideways.

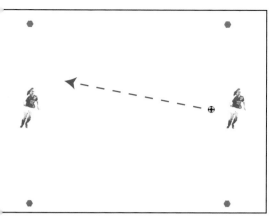

Goalkeeper practice 3 – handling.

Goalkeeper practice 3

- There are two goalkeepers with a number of footballs in an area approximately 15 yards long × 10 yards wide.
- Each goalkeeper is to defend a goal approximately 6 yards wide.

- They take it in turns to serve the ball at each other, on the ground, at waist, chest and head height, above head height.
- The service should preferably be a half-volley at a match pace.

Goalkeeper practice 4

- There are two goalkeepers with a supply of footballs approximately 20 yards apart.
- There is a short row of marker discs and a goal about 6 yards wide.
- The goalkeeper uses her footwork to move forward towards the goal, where she sets ready to receive the ball.
- As the working goalkeeper sets, the other goalkeeper serves the ball towards the goal at match pace.

Goalkeeper practice 5

- The practice takes place in an area approximately 10 yards × 10 yards. There are two servers and one working goalkeeper, who works sideways from disc to disc.
- As the goalkeeper reaches the disc she sets ready to receive the ball and the server serves the ball at the goalkeeper.
- The service should be varied and at match pace.

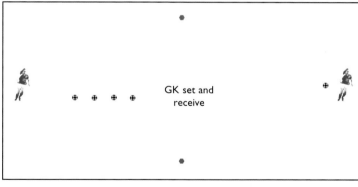

GK set and receive

Goalkeeper practice 4 – footwork and handling.

Goalkeeper practice 5 – footwork and handling.

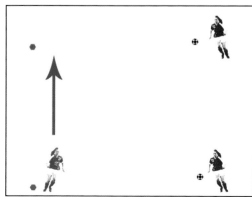

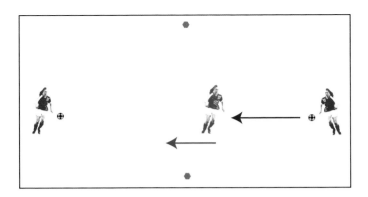

Goalkeeper practice 6 – footwork and handling.

Goalkeeper practice 6

- There are two servers and one goalkeeper, who works in a centrally located goal about 6 yards wide. The servers are approximately 10 yards away from the goal on opposite sides.
- The goalkeeper faces one of the servers and defends the goal.
- The first server serves the ball at the goalkeeper, service should be varied and at match pace.
- The goalkeeper receives the ball, rolls it back to the server, then turns and sets ready to receive the next ball.

Shot Stopping and Saving the Ball

Angles and distances are important judgements for the goalkeeper to make and will vary from individual to individual. However, it is vital that she continually adjusts as the ball moves, in order to maintain a good position and keep the illusion of a small, well-defended target.

Moving Into Line

The goalkeeper's first consideration is always to move into line with the ball and the goal. Put simply, if an imaginary triangle was to be drawn between the ball and the two goal-posts, the goalkeeper should always try to position herself on the centre line formed by the ball.

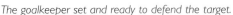

The goalkeeper set and ready to defend the target.

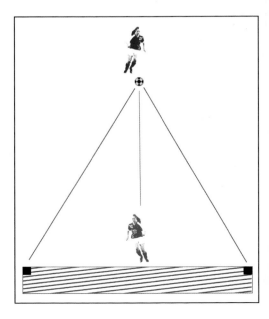

Goalkeeper positioning with the ball in a central area.

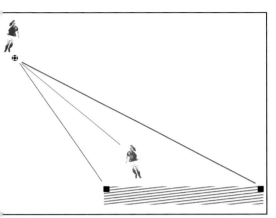

Goalkeeper positioning with the ball in a wide area.

When the ball is in a wide area, the near post becomes more vulnerable than the far post; therefore, the goalkeeper should ensure that the near post can be covered by taking no more than one step. The far post is then covered by a step and a dive.

Moving Down the Line

Having moved into line with the ball, the goalkeeper should attempt to move down the line in order to narrow the angle. She should watch the player with the ball carefully as she moves, being ready to stop and set as the player takes the shot. Her distance off the goal line is determined by the position of the ball, her size and the quality of the opposition. It is a fine judgement and one that is individual to each goalkeeper.

Diving

If it is not possible to move into the line of the ball, then the goalkeeper will have to dive in order to make the save.

- She should push off with the leg nearest the ball.
- Lead with the hands, which should be together.
- Dive forwards towards the ball in order to take it early.
- The hand nearest the ball should be directly behind it to provide the first barrier.
- The eyes should watch the ball all the way into her hands.
- Impact with the ground should be from the hips and the shoulder, not the elbow, as this can dislodge the ball.
- The ball is trapped and gathered into the body to make it safe.
- If the ball cannot be held, then it should be deflected away using the open palm of the nearest hand.

Collapsing Saves (see photo on page 126)

This technique is to be used for a ball that is moving on the ground, immediately to the side of the body. If the ball is moving at pace, and footwork into line isn't possible, the body should collapse on to the ball in order to make the save.

- The goalkeeper should be set and crouched low, with her hands out in front of her.
- As she reaches for the ball, her legs should collapse behind her.
- The ball is secured and trapped into the chest.

Diving forwards and leading with the hands.

Making the ball safe.

A collapsing save.

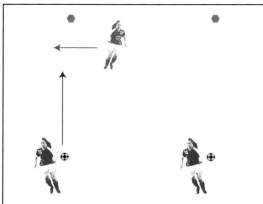

Goalkeeper practice 7 – diving saves.

Simple Practices to Improve Shot Stopping
Goalkeeper practice 7
- The goalkeeper sets out two marker discs about 6 yards apart.
- There are two servers with a ball each who stand 10 yards away from each disc.
- The goalkeeper crouches in the middle of the target ready to dive or collapse.
- The first server bounces the ball as a signal to the goalkeeper and then serves the ball towards the marker disc. This can be kicked on the ground for a collapsing save or thrown for a diving save.
- Repeat on the other side.

A simple progression to this practice for a more advanced goalkeeper would be:

- The goalkeeper begins in the centre of the target with her back to the servers. On the command she turns, advances, sets and reacts to the service to make the save.

Goalkeeper practice 8
- There are two 6-yard goals about 10 yards apart and two goalkeepers with a supply of footballs behind each target.
- The goalkeepers take it in turns to try and score past each other.

TOP TIP

When coaching diving and collapsing saves the coach should look out for the goalkeeper taking off from the wrong foot and leading with the wrong hand.

- The service should be varied and at match pace.
Goalkeeper practice 9
- Six small goals about 2 yards across and set out as shown in the diagram opposite.
- There is one working goalkeeper and a server who face each other about 6 yards apart at one end of the grid.
- The server throws the ball for the goalkeeper to make a collapsing or diving save before it goes through target 1.
- The ball is rolled back to the server, who moves backwards ready to serve into target 2.

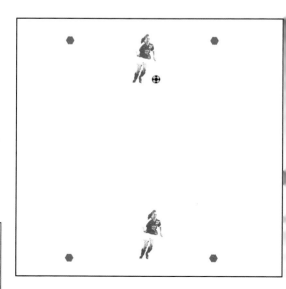

Goalkeeper practice 8 – duel.

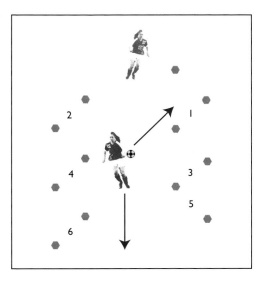

Goalkeeper practice 9 – diving and collapsing technique.

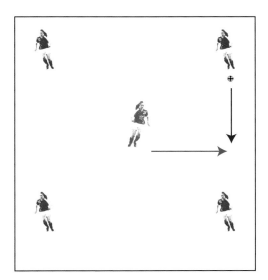

Goalkeeper practice 10 – intercepting the ball.

The goalkeeper moves to defend target 2 and saves the ball, as before.

Goalkeeper practice 10

Four outfield players organize themselves on to the corners of a 10-yard square. The goalkeeper is positioned in the middle of this square.

The servers pass the ball to each other on the ground.

The goalkeeper must dive or collapse to intercept and win the ball.

Goalkeeper practice 11

There is one full-sized goal, three outfield players to act as servers, who have a ball each. The servers are located about 15 yards from the goal line in central and wide areas.

- The goalkeeper starts with her back to the post, looking towards the corner flag.
- On the command 'play' she moves quickly into line and then down the line until she has to set and save the shot.
- The ball is rolled back to the server.
- The goalkeeper retreats towards the centre of the goal to start again with the central player.

Variation

The servers have one ball between them, which is passed from one to the other, making the goalkeeper continually adjust her position in relation to the ball. Upon receiving the ball, the server can shoot or pass it on.

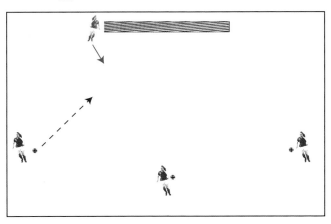

Goalkeeper practice 11 – getting into line and down the line.

Dealing with Crosses and High Balls

This aspect of the goalkeeper's role is arguably the most difficult for the female goalkeeper to master. For consistent success she needs to show continued good judgement, sound technique, as well as being brave enough to leave her goal-line in order to attack the ball through a mêlée of players.

Positioning

- The goalkeeper should be 4–6 yards off her goal-line in the middle to the back-half of her goal.
- Her stance should be open, which means that she can see the ball but also watch the movements of the outfield players in more central areas of the pitch.

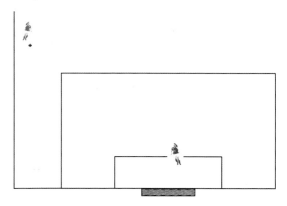

Ball in a wide position outside the penalty area.

- As the ball moves down the wing towards the goal-line, the goalkeeper should adjust her position back towards her goal.
- She takes up a position in the middle of the goal, about 2 yards off her goal-line.
- Her stance should be open.

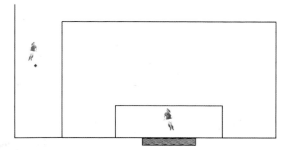

Ball in a wide position up to 18 yards from the goal-line.

- If the ball continues to move towards the goal-line the goalkeeper should begin to edge towards the front-half of her goal.
- As the ball travels into the penalty area, the goalkeeper should adjust her position towards the front post.
- She should be approximately 1 yard off her goal-line with an open stance.
- She should be ready to defend the front post, as well as deal with any shots resulting from the ball being cut back towards the penalty spot.

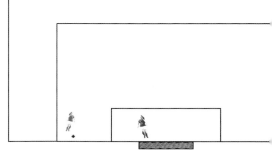

Ball in a wide position inside the penalty area.

- The goalkeeper should position herself in the middle to back-half of her goal, approximately 1–2 yards off her goal-line.
- Her stance should be open and ready to defend the ball into the goal area.

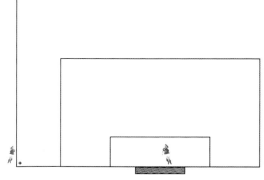

Positioning for corners.

Catching the Ball

There is no reason for the goalkeeper to move before the ball is kicked and in the air; therefore, she should:

Wait and move late.

As the ball is in the air, she should assess the flight – its line, its pace and its trajectory.

Decide and adjust her position:

- If the decision is to go to the ball, she should move out into its line quickly to provide the momentum to jump and catch the ball.
- If the decision is to stay and defend the goal, she should adjust her position to deal with the anticipated shot on goal.

Secure the ball:

- The goalkeeper jumps whilst she is moving into line with the ball. Take-off is from either leg, with the other bending to help momentum and provide stability.
- Her hands are outstretched, reaching forwards for the ball. She catches it in front of her head, at the highest point of her jump and with her hands in the 'W' position.
- The goalkeeper's head is steady and her eyes watch the ball all the way into her hands.

Note: It is best to try to catch the ball whenever possible, although there are situations when the ball should be punched clear or deflected to safety (see photo on page 130):

- There is a strong challenge from a number of opponents.
- The ball is too high and the goalkeeper is off-balance.
- The goalkeeper is moving backwards towards her goal.

TOP TIP

Common problems that the coach will encounter when working to develop dealing with crosses and high balls:

- The goalkeeper is closed to play.
- The goalkeeper is drawn towards the ball.
- The goalkeeper moves too early when attacking the ball.

Sunderland's Helen Alderson comfortably gathers a cross.

Coming to punch the ball through a mêlée of players.

Simple Practices to Improve a Goalkeeper Dealing with Crosses

When setting up practices to develop these techniques, the quality and consistency of the service is important in order that the goalkeeper can achieve repeated practice. Service can be thrown (using a throw-in technique to mimic the flight of the ball) or volleyed, if necessary.

Goalkeeper practice 12

- There are two goalkeepers with a ball between them.
- One goalkeeper stands about 2 yards behind the serving goalkeeper.
- The server throws the ball into the air above her head.
- The goalkeeper moves forward and jumps to catch the ball.

Goalkeeper practice 13

- Three servers with a ball each stand with their backs to the working goalkeeper, who is about 4 yards behind the servers.
- Each server is numbered 1 to 3 and, as her number is called, she throws her ball into the air above her head.
- The working goalkeeper moves forward and jumps to catch the ball.

Goalkeeper practice 14

- Player 1 begins with the ball in a wide area. She takes a touch out of her feet and crosses the ball.
- The goalkeeper catches the ball, then distributes it to player 2.
- The practice begins again from the opposite wing.

Goalkeeper practice 12 – introduction to catching a high ball.

Variation

Another player is added to the practice. She is located in front of the goalkeeper and acts as a passive target for the crossed ball.

Goalkeeper practice 13 – catching a high ball.

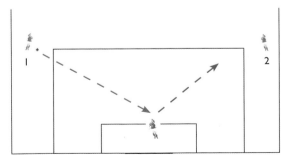

Goalkeeper practice 14 – dealing with the crossed ball.

Distribution

As well as being the last line of defence, the modern goalkeeper is also the first line of the attack, meaning that she must be as competent with her feet as any outfield player. She has to be able to deal with through balls and back passes, as well as distribute the ball accurately and effectively after it is safely in her possession.

Throwing the Ball
- Rolling the ball. This is the best technique for moving the ball quickly over a short distance.
- Over-arm throws. For longer distances, the goalkeeper can use a bowling action to propel the ball. The ball should be released at the top of the arc, as shown in the photo below.
- Javelin throws. The over-arm throw can travel long distances but tends to have a looped trajec-

tory; therefore, to get the ball straight to a team-mate with a flatter trajectory the javelin throw is more appropriate.

Kicking Techniques
If there is no quick-throwing option available to the goalkeeper, or the team strategy prefers the ball to be kicked over longer distances, then a volley from her hands or a simple long, lofted pass from outside the penalty area is her best option.

- The ball is held in front of the goalkeeper's body.
- She moves forward and drops the ball towards her kicking foot.
- The ankle is locked and contact is through the underside of the ball with the laces of the boot.
- She watches the ball on to her foot and follows through.

Rachel Brown throws the ball out to a team-mate.

Rolling the ball out.

Karen Bardsley guards her post.

The Goalkeeper in the Game

It is very important that the goalkeeper remains involved in the game wherever the ball is located on the pitch. Her presence behind the back line provides impact on the game and ensures that her team-mates are confident in her abilities.

- Starting position.
  By continually adjusting her position in relation to the location of the ball, the goalkeeper maintains her concentration, remains focused and is able to deal with each situation as it unfolds.
- Communication.
  Verbal communication is a large part of the goalkeeper's role; it should be clear, concise and calm, using words that are both positive and informative to her team-mates. A verbal goalkeeper is also concentrating on the game and contributing to the overall confidence of the team.
- Decisive.
  The goalkeeper must make decisions and then act on them. Hesitancy or a change of mind will breed uncertainty and affect the confidence of the team.

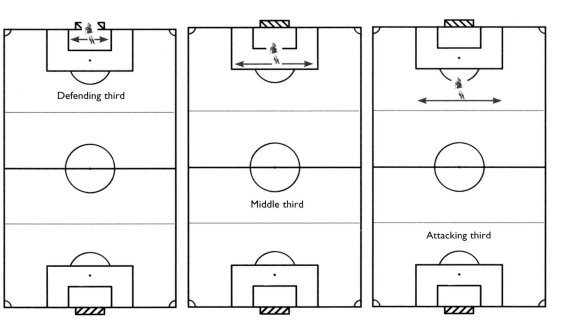

Goalkeeper's positioning off her line when the ball is in the defending third.

Goalkeeper's positioning off her line when the ball is in the middle third.

Goalkeeper's positioning off her line when the ball is in the attacking third.

CHAPTER 9

STRATEGIES AND TACTICS FOR THE WOMEN'S GAME

At one level, football is a simple competition between two teams of eleven players, with the winner being decided by whichever team scores the most goals. However, if a team wishes to have sustained success, then they must have a playing strategy; this is essentially a plan that provides the players with broad guidelines to help them to defend and to attack effectively.

The strategy is the starting point from which the team tactics are developed; it is the tactics that provide the finer details, defining more precisely the role of each unit and each individual within that unit.

Successful teams are not only characterized by individuality, spontaneity and unpredictability, but they also have knowledgeable players who are capable of making informed decisions based on a thorough understanding of the playing strategy. Effective tactical development often treads a fine line between structure and freedom because players should be allowed to make mistakes and then empowered to find their own solutions following these mistakes. If they become accustomed to the coach providing all the answers, they will not develop the skills required to adapt to the challenges and conflicts within the game.

The Playing Strategy

A team's strategy will be strongly influenced by the beliefs and philosophy of the coach behind it. However, the ideas within the strategy should be both suitable and realistic for the level at which the team competes; they should also be adapted to suit the ability of the players, having fully taken into account the overall strengths and weaknesses of the squad.

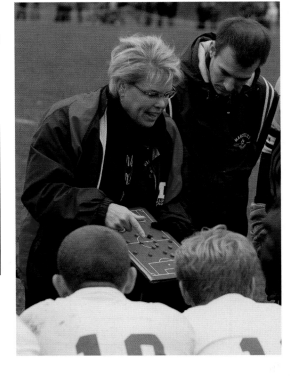

> **TOP TIP**
>
> As a general rule:
>
> - Devise a clear and simple strategy for both attack and defence.
> - Decide how it will be communicated, implemented and reinforced throughout the season.
> - Provide the players with the freedom and confidence to make their own decisions within the confines of the playing strategy.

LEFT: *Sunset over the Andes during the Under-20s World Cup in Chile.*

RIGHT: *Half-time team talk.*

Strategic Fundamentals

Whatever strategy is to be employed, it is convenient to split the pitch into separate areas where the strategic priorities can be outlined in a simple manner.

Typical Considerations for a Defensive Strategy

- Which areas of the pitch are the most vulnerable and, therefore, have to be defended by the strongest means possible?
- Which areas of the pitch are the least vulnerable and where can space be safely conceded to the opposition?
- Is the team is going to defend high and press early, or concede space by dropping deep and putting maximum numbers between the ball and the goal?

Attacking Third

A good defending strategy relates to all areas of the pitch. In the example below, delay is listed as a priority. Strikers will be expected to discourage quick, forward

play, which provides time for the rest of the team to recover behind the ball and regain its defensive shape.

Middle Third

Delay, shape and patience will allow the team to become compact, thereby restricting space and discouraging penetrating forward passes. Players are encouraged to pressurize and win the ball in this third, if the right moment presents itself. Forward runs by the opposition midfield players must be tracked.

Defending Third

Spaces in the vulnerable areas around the goal are covered in order to make forward play and shots on goal difficult. The player with the ball should be immediately pressurized; tackling to win the ball is a high priority. Players must also be tightly marked and runners tracked.

Defensive Styles of Play

High-Pressure Defending

This is a very aggressive and physical style of play relying on individuals winning the ball back, or forcing errors as early and as high up the pitch as possible. Such a style requires a high back line and will possibly employ an offside trap.

Low-Pressure Defending

When possession is lost, the team will retreat back towards its own defending third, putting bodies between the ball and the goal. There will be a predetermined line of pressure and, once the ball crosses this, the team will try to win the ball back.

Zonal Defending and a Compact Team Shape

A compact shape restricts the available space in key areas, whilst zonal responsibilities ensure that there is cover, support and balance throughout the entire team. Response is quick wherever the ball is moved to and the movement of the opposition players is tracked and countered.

Individual Marking with Partial Zonal Defending

Key members of the opposition are marked individually to deny them time and space on the ball, whilst the rest of the team defends zonally.

Typical Considerations for an Attacking Strategy

- What are the key areas through which the team will attack (central, wide or both)?

Defending third — Aggressive pressure / Tight marking / Restrict space / Restrict goal scoring opportunities / Win the ball

Direction of play

Middle third — Restricting forward passes / Marking and covering / Recovery and shape / Tracking runners / Delay and pressure

Attacking third — Delay / Recovery / Regain shape

Typical priorities in defence.

- How will goal-scoring opportunities be created? Perhaps there will be build-up play through the midfield or more reliance on direct play, which utilizes long passes and quick support from the midfield.

Defending Third
When the ball is regained, possession must be secured by passing to a player with time and space; this could be back to the goalkeeper or across to the defence. As this happens, the team begins to spread out into its attacking positions.

Middle Third
Most teams will aim to establish their attacking pattern in the middle third. This will involve movement to secure the ball, movement to maintain possession, as well as movement to provide forward-passing opportunities.

Attacking Third
Movement and passing should have one aim, to create goal scoring opportunities. Passes should look to penetrate behind the defence, pressurize the goalkeeper and create enough space to be able to take a shot at goal.

Attacking Styles of Play

Direct Play
This is a very aggressive attacking style suitable for teams that play with a high-pressure defence. Once the ball is regained, the team's aim is to create goal-scoring opportunities by getting it into the attacking third as early as possible.

Counter-Attacking
This is a slightly more sophisticated attacking style than direct play, as it relies on the opposition being lured into advanced positions. When they give the ball away, they are hit on the counter-attack and the ball is moved forward quickly, whilst they are out of position. A low-pressure defensive strategy would suit this style of play.

Systematic Build-Up
Here possession is maintained for long periods, whilst the team moves forward and the opposition is probed for weakness. It often involves a slow, patient build-up, with an explosive change of pace once an opportunity to penetrate into the attacking third is found. Teams organized for zonal defending lend themselves to this style of attack because it is equally reliant on team shape to exploit vulnerable areas of the pitch.

Formation Fundamentals

There is much debate within football about the merits of different types of playing formation, but essentially all a formation does is to provide a quick and convenient way to organize eleven players into units on the pitch. Undoubtedly different formations lend themselves to certain strategies and playing styles, but it is the level of each player's understanding that ultimately makes the difference between a cohesive and successful team performance or a disjointed failure.

The 4–4–2: Four Defenders–Four Midfielders–Two Attackers

- The 4–4–2 and its variations are the most popular playing systems throughout the world.
- It is a strong, defensive formation with two ranks of four located centrally in front of the goal.
- This formation is very effective across the full width of the pitch because of the two ranks of four players.
- The symmetrical nature of the formation allows an easy rotation of roles between individuals.

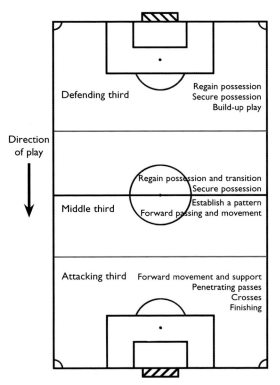

Typical priorities in attack.

In this France v USA Under-20 international, the shape and playing formation of both teams is clearly identifiable.

This lends itself to flexibility in attack and a quick recovery in defence.
- In attack, the forwards are reliant on quick support from central and wide midfield positions.

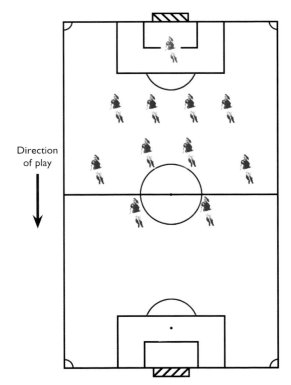

Direction of play

The 4–4–2.

The 4–3–3: Four Defenders–Three Midfielders–Three Attackers

- This is an attacking formation that has been used with success, primarily by the USA women's team.
- The forward line automatically provides width in the attacking third and immediate pressure on the opposition defenders, once the ball is lost.
- The midfield triangle can be organized as shown in the left-hand diagram on page 139, with two defensive players and one attacking midfielder, or inverted to provide two attacking players and one defender.
- Movement, rotation and support between forwards and advanced midfielders are features of the attack.
- The back four primarily have a defensive role and play little part in an attacking move, once the ball is in the opposition's half.

The 3–5–2: Three Defenders–Five Midfielders–Two Attackers

- This is an attacking formation that relies on a strong midfield. It has been used effectively at international level by Brazil.
- The three defenders and the deep midfielder provide defensive strength in the central area of the defending and middle thirds, but they inevitably concede space on the flanks.
- The wide midfield players provide width in attack through the middle and attacking thirds, without weakening the centre of the field.

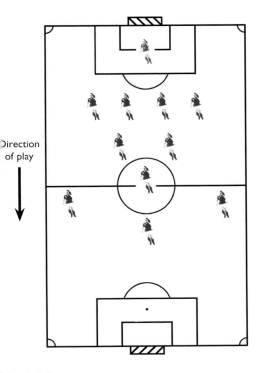

The 4–3–3.

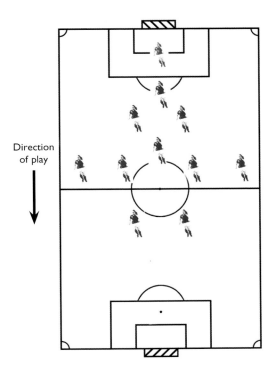

The 3–5–2.

Tactical Considerations

The Defensive Unit: the Back Four

The back four can be organized to defend either zonally, across the width of the pitch, or as a line of three players supported from behind by a sweeper.

Zonal Defending

A zonal defence will typically have two aggressive, ball-winning central defenders and two quick, mobile full backs: one on the right flank and one on the left. The goalkeeper supports the unit from behind and her positioning off the goal-line allows her to cover any long, forward balls that are played behind the defence. Her verbal instruction fine-tunes the unit's positioning and this role has given rise to the term 'sweeper keeper' in recent years.

To be effective, zonal defence has to be well-drilled, as it requires each of the four players to respond in unison to the ball as it moves up and down, as well as across, the pitch. The defensive principles of pressure, cover, balance and compactness are the keys to success with distances between each player and each unit being crucial elements in the restriction of space.

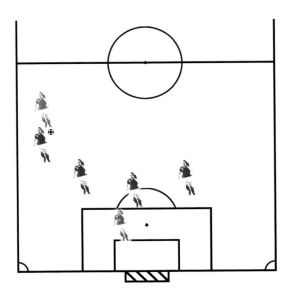

Shape of the zonal back four with the ball in a wide position.

- The overall width of the unit from full-back to full-back should be about 40 yards.
- Space is conceded on the right flank, where there is little immediate danger.
- The shape and depth of the unit encourage the ball to be played in front, rather than behind them.
- The first defender, the left full-back, is pressing the ball and forcing play inside to where the unit is strongest.
- The second defender is providing cover. She should be open to play and ready to press should the first defender be beaten.
- The third defender is open to play and providing deeper cover. She should be aware of the movement of the opposition forwards and be ready to track any runs across the front of her.
- The fourth defender provides balance. She is open to play and ready to track any runners from wide areas. She is approximately in line with the back post.
- The goalkeeper is off her goal-line and in line with the ball and the centre of her goal. She is open to play, on her toes and ready to react to the long, diagonal ball to the back of the defence.
- The overall width of the unit from full-back to full-back should be about 40 yards.
- Space is conceded on either flank, where there is little immediate danger.

- The shape and depth of the unit encourage the ball to be played in front, rather than behind them.
- The first defender, the left-central defender, is pressing the ball and forcing play inside to where the unit is strongest.
- The second defenders are providing cover. Both are open to play and ready to press should the first defender be beaten, or track any runs by opposition attackers across the front of them.
- Note that there are two second defenders: the left-back and the right-central defenders.
- The third defender is open to play and providing deeper cover and balance. She should be aware of the movement of the opposition forwards and be ready to track any runs across the front of her.
- The goalkeeper is off the goal-line and in line with the ball and the centre of the goal. She is open to play, on her toes and ready to react to the long ball to the back of the defence.

A Back Four with a Sweeper

This is a variation on a zonal back four and would be a simple way of defending against a front three. Each defender has individual responsibility for their immediate opponent, whilst the sweeper has the freedom to defend balls played into channels and behind the defence. The goalkeeper would take up a deeper position and have a reduced outfield role.

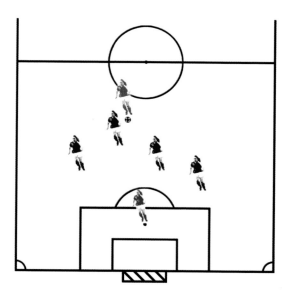

Shape of the zonal back four with the ball in a central position.

The back four with a sweeper.

A central defender designated as a sweeper must be able to read the game, as well as respond quickly to penetrating forward passes and crosses. She is also an asset in attack, as she generally has time on the ball and can see the whole pitch, which gives her time to make the right decision.

Some teams also choose to play a back four with a sweeper and three zonal defenders. In these instances they would have to be tucked into closer positions than a normal back four, and be more willing to sacrifice ground on the flanks in order to keep the central area tight and to restrict goal-scoring opportunities.

The Defensive Unit: the Back Three

A back three is normally deployed as two out-and-out markers supported by a sweeper behind and a deep-lying goalkeeper. Players in this system would primarily be defenders, with little expectation of joining in with an attacking move.

The two marking players are generally uncompromising and aggressive 1 v 1 defenders. They should remain tight, restrict space, prevent turns and limit shooting opportunities. Their primary role is to win the ball.

A back three is vulnerable to channel balls and flank play, but simple to organize. It provides strength in the centre of the pitch and allows another player to be deployed in an advanced position elsewhere on the pitch.

The Attacking Unit

For many coaches games are won and lost in midfield, hence this unit, no matter what formation is played, would have a key role in both defence and attack. The offensive formation varies enormously according to the team's strategic aims but in all cases will rely on the simple attacking principles of creating and then exploiting space.

Diamond in Midfield

Midfielder a. Primarily a defensive central midfielder who would act as a 'playmaker' linking with the defence in build-up play and providing longer passes that penetrate behind the opposition.
Midfielder b. The wide midfield play infield, away from the line to provide space for the full-backs to overlap or support behind.
Midfielder c. Supporting runs from deeper positions and often in advance of the forwards are difficult to track and mark.

Rotation in Midfield (see page 142)

In this variation of a 4–4–2, there is still one defensive central midfielder as previously described, but here there is more emphasis on an attack through the wings via the wide midfielders and the full-backs who provide support from behind.

In the centre, a rotation of roles between the midfield and the striker both creates and exploits space in front of the opposition defenders.

Attacking in a 4–3–3 (see page 142)

In attack, the wingers and centre-forward would push high to fully occupy the opposition back line, whilst the remaining central midfielder would look to support play from a deeper position. The full-backs would provide support to the attacking move from behind.

When the ball is lost, the defensive block formed by the two central defenders and the two central midfielders protects the central space and restricts passing options up to the feet of the opposition forwards.

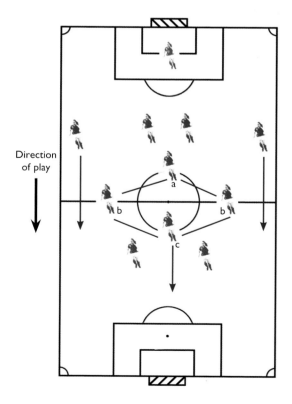

Direction of play

A diamond midfield in a 4–4–2.

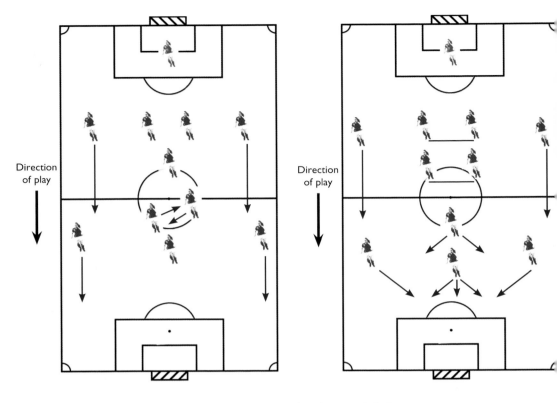

A 4–4–2 in defence converts into a 4–1–2–3 in attack.

Attacking in a 4–3–3.

Playing Styles in the Women's Game

A study of international playing styles shows a variety of approaches by the world's top-ranked teams, although in most cases this is generally linked to the wider football philosophy that is prevalent in their geographical region.

The USA has dominated international women's football since the first Women's World Cup in 1991. However, although they have a huge playing pool from which to select, football plays only a minor role in their wider sporting culture. Their playing style relies less on technical finesse and more on an imposing physical presence that is supported by an indomitable self-belief. They often line up with a front three and their success to date has been primarily based on a high-tempo, direct playing style, which tends to out-power the opposition.

In Europe, where football has a stronger cultural influence, teams are highly organized and players show a more instinctive appreciation for the nuances of the game. The Germans have successfully challenged the USA by employing a playing style that is not only highly organized, but characterized by players who have high levels of both technical ability and tactical understanding. They derive their strength from a solid and well-drilled defensive strategy that switches seamlessly into an attacking formation once the ball is regained. They use rotation and high-quality movement to create space, which provides a variety of attacking options from all areas of the pitch.

In Brazil, the game is played in a more instinctive fashion with great emphasis being placed on an individual player's ability to 'dazzle'. To date their progress has been based around the technical qualities of a core group who emerged during the first Under-19 World Championships in 2002, It will be interesting to see whether their momentum can be maintained once these players begin to be replaced.

Arguably it is Japan where the most interesting, female-friendly developments have taken place; they have steadily climbed the world rankings to become an important women's football nation. Their teams are characterized by an extremely high work-rate with a defensive strategy that relies on a high tempo and committed pressure through the middle- and defending-thirds. In attack they play off a limited number of touches moving the ball neatly and intricately up the pitch. Short passing, quick combinations and good off-the-ball movement have proved to be effective at all international age-groups and seem well-suited to the female psyche.

It is important to look at the trends internationally in order to help the domestic game to develop, although here it is perhaps more appropriate to adapt the playing style not only to the general attributes of the female player, but also to the specific characteristics of the team involved. Coaches should consider the following points:

- **The size of the pitch and the goal**. Women's football is played in areas that are sized for their male counterparts, which of course places an extra physical burden on the female player. The physical demands of a playing strategy should be considered carefully and measured against the physical capacity of the individuals expected to carry out high-volume roles. For example, in a 3–5–2 it could be unrealistic to expect the two wide-midfield players to operate up and down the full length of the pitch at a consistently high tempo for the full 90 minutes.
- **Physical size and strength**. Female players are on average smaller and less powerful than male players, which has an impact on the pace at which the game can be played. Build-up play is generally slower and long balls are consistently less accurate, especially when technique has not been adequately perfected. This affects the quality of crosses, makes a quick switch of play from flank to flank more difficult and also acts as a hindrance to a direct, counter-attacking playing strategy. Size is also an issue for goalkeepers and a characteristic of the women's game at all levels is the number of goals that are scored from looping, long-range shots that dip over the goalkeeper and into the net. Because of this positioning off the goal-line, as well as presence in the goal, is an important factor that all female goalkeepers and their coaches should carefully consider.
- **Team-orientated**. As discussed in Chapter 4, female players tend to place a greater emphasis on their role within a team than their male counterparts. In general, she needs to fit in and has an inbuilt eagerness to play her part in the team along with an unwillingness to appear either selfish or aggressive. Overall this could perhaps mean that a women's team is best suited to co-operative strategies; for example, an attack based around the principles of possession and a defence employing zonal tactics.

> **TOP TIP**
>
> Undoubtedly there are distinct differences in the way women play football, although that doesn't mean that the game should be coached any differently, nor should strategies that rely on high levels of physical prowess be ignored. The coach merely has to adapt ideas and moderate expectations in order to obtain the desired results.

The USA making friends in Chile.

CHAPTER 10

FITNESS FOR FOOTBALL

Football is an intensely physical activity, the game is demanding and the season is long, with games being played not only in the coldest weather, but also on heavy, muddy pitches. Most women are amateur players and have to juggle home and work with training, travelling and playing. Good physical conditioning, therefore, is important if a player is to cope with the demands that are placed on her on a day-to-day basis.

As well as a good level of fitness, she also needs to know about:

Efficient recovery strategies following games or training sessions.
Exercises that minimize the risk from injury.
Diet and hydration to support a healthy sporting lifestyle.
Medical issues for the female athlete.

Physical Conditioning

Football is a high-intensity, intermittent activity. Research by sports scientists has found that the game places the following demands on the average female player:

- A women's international midfield player covers approximately 7 miles (11km) during an average game.
- A combination league midfield player covers approximately 4.5 miles (7km) during an average game.
- Physical activities by percentage:
  - 44 per cent walking.
  - 32 per cent jogging.
  - 13 per cent static.
  - 10 per cent striding.
  - 1 per cent sprinting flat-out. Although this seems quite low in comparison to the other percentages, it is actually approximately 100 × 5-yard (5m) sprints.
- Jumping, falling and tackling should be added to the above as being typically repeated activities throughout the game.

LEFT: Warming up as a team-building activity.

RIGHT: Casey Stoney and Rachel Yankey in a pre-game warm-up.

THE BENEFITS OF A SIMPLE CONDITIONING PROGRAMME

- Promotes cardio-respiratory efficiency, which increases blood flow and oxygen supply to the muscles.
- Burns fat.
- Aids recovery and minimises the effects of muscle soreness following the activity.

It is quite clear from these statistics that physical preparation is important for the female player, no matter at what level she competes. Training should aim to improve both aerobic and anaerobic endurance. The development of aerobic endurance will ensure that the player can work repeatedly for longer periods of the game, whilst the development of anaerobic endurance will ensure that the player can work explosively throughout the duration of the game.

Conditioning activities can be easily incorporated into the weekly training programme, and to keep the players motivated the sessions should be:

- Varied and specific to football.
- Involve a ball as much as possible.
- Measurable to allow the players to see, as well as feel, that they are progressing.
- Challenging, although individuals should only compete against themselves, as it is unrealistic to pick out the best performer and expect every member of the team to achieve her standards.

There are two simple tests of endurance that require a minimal amount of equipment and that can be easily implemented by amateur teams and players. Either of these should be undertaken at the start of the season then repeated every 8 to 10 weeks, keeping the testing conditions as consistent as possible in order to provide a realistic comparison of the results over the season.

- The Cooper Test. Players run as far as possible for a period of 12 minutes and the individual results are then recorded.
- The Bleep test. This is a shuttle test, which should be run over a marked, non-slip 20m distance. It requires a CD and player but is a commonly used testing method that would allow an easy comparison of results from a number of sources.

Simple Aerobic Endurance Sessions

Some players are able to accurately monitor their training heart-rate by using a personal heart-rate monitor. This will ensure that she works at the appropriate level in order to gain maximum benefit from the session. However, for the purposes of this volume, it is sufficient to state that the player should work as hard as she can for as long as she can during the conditioning session.

Aerobic development can be either one continuous activity or an interval-training session, where the players undertake high-tempo activities, as timed sets with timed breaks between sets.

Following a warm-up, a continuous activity should last for about 20 minutes, whilst an interval-training session should contain at least 15 minutes of actual activity.

The Small-Sided Game

This type of session is an ideal method to develop aerobic fitness in the players, as they spend the time playing football without realizing the physiological benefits of the game. The organization and timing, however, are important if there are to be any lasting benefits from this type of work:

Conditioning circuit.

ypical activities in a mixed
erobic circuit.

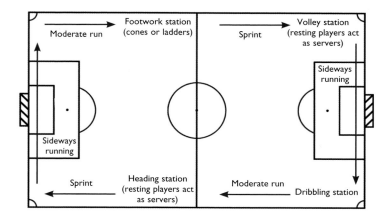

The squad should be split into four teams of three players. Two teams rest and two teams work.
The resting teams are located around the marked playing area and will feed the ball back in to the area when it goes out, in order to keep the playing tempo high.
The playing area should be at least 20 × 30 yards with a small target on either end line.
Play is directional and the ball should be stopped in the target area in order to score a goal.
Play is continuous during the specified time period; there should be no breaks and no coaching.
Each game and rest should be to a 1:1 ratio. For example, a playing time of 4 minutes would be followed by a resting time of 4 minutes.

Mixed Circuit

This could be organized as an interval session or one continuous run. A range of football-specific activity locations are set out at different points in a circuit. The players then work around the circuit for the specified length of time, undertaking each of the activities as they get to them. If the session is conducted as an interval session, the work-to-rest ratio should be 1:1 and, as in the previous example, 4 minutes work to 4 minutes rest repeated for a number of sets would be ideal.

Simple Anaerobic and Speed-Development Sessions

Players should work at full pace in every repetition in order to gain any benefit from these activities; this especially means that quality is more important than quantity.
Circuits should never be in a straight line and should be devised to provide 5–10 seconds of work for the individual. The work-to-rest ratio should be at least

1:5 in order to ensure a full recovery before the player undertakes the next repetition.
A speed-development session could easily be slotted into 10 minutes at the end of the warm-up and there should also be some time set aside for stretching after the session has finished.

Speed Development
- Two players start side by side. On the coach's command, they race to the finish via their gate.
- The players should be passing a ball to each other at the start or there could be a static start from a sitting, lying or turning position.

Gate Race
- Six 1-yard gates are randomly placed in front of the players.
- P1 sets off first and must run through each gate and then on to the finish.
- P2 follows after P1 has gone through the same gate. She must follow the same path as P1 but try to catch her before she finishes.

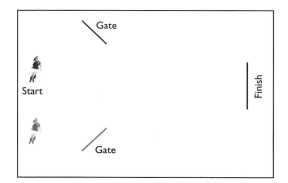

Speed development.

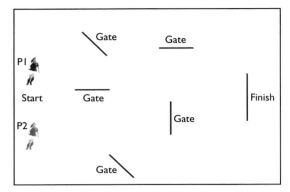

Speed development – gate race.

The Importance of Warm-Up and Cool-Down

Every session should begin with a warm-up and end with a cool-down, as both activities provide a period of transition for the body from its resting to its active state and vice versa.

The benefits of a good warm-up are:

- The heart rate is gradually increased as the body becomes used to the exercise.
- Internal body and muscle temperatures are raised, which stimulates the elasticity within the muscles and helps to reduce the risk of strains from over-stretching.
- Blood flow is stimulated, which deposits oxygen around the body and assists athletic performance.

- The warm-up provides time to prepare mentally and provides focus for the activity to come.

Warm-ups should be tailored to suit the work that is to follow, but typically the first 12–15 minutes of any warm-up must include the following:

- Jogging (5–10 minutes' duration). This activity can be undertaken with or without the ball, including running forwards, backwards and sideways, as well as heel flicks and knee raises.
- Dynamic stretching (5–10 minutes' duration). Dynamic stretches mimic the movements of the game and are undertaken whilst the player is moving over a distance of 10–20 yards (9–18m). The action stimulates the neural pathways, works the heart and prepares the body far more effectively than static stretches. The other benefit is that players can work together as a group in a rhythmical and co-ordinated fashion, which provides mental outcomes for the activity, as well as the obvious physical ones.

Basic Dynamic Stretches

Knee Lifts – Stretches Gluteals and Hamstrings
The player drives one knee upwards towards her chest, then takes two steps before driving the other knee towards her chest. This is repeated over a short distance.

Straight-Leg Kicks – Stretches the Hamstrings
The player takes a controlled kick in front of her body and, keeping the leg as straight as possible, she then

Knee lifts.

Straight-leg kicks.

akes two steps before kicking the other leg. This is repeated over a short distance.

Side-Leg Kicks – Stretches the Groin and the Hamstrings

The player takes a controlled kick across the front of her body, whilst twisting her shoulders in the opposite direction. She then takes two steps before kicking the other leg. This is repeated over a short distance.

Groin Stretch #1 – Stretches the Groin

The player lifts one knee and opens out the groin towards the outside of her body. She then takes two steps before repeating with the other leg.

Groin Stretch #2 – Stretches the Groin

The player opens out her leg, lifts the knee and brings it round to the front of her body. She then takes two steps before repeating with the other leg.

The cool-down returns the body to its resting state, lowering the heart rate, removing waste products from the muscles and so helping to minimize the onset of stiffness over the next 48 hours. It is the first step towards recovery following the session or game and would involve jogging, which gradually slows to a walk, and dynamic stretches. Further recovery strategies for the more committed players would include an ice bath, wearing compression garments on the legs, refuelling, re-hydrating and a good rest.

The Training Programme

A comprehensive training programme, which will develop all-round fitness for football, should include strength training, development of flexibility and plyometrics to develop explosive power. These activities all require the player to learn techniques that are best taught by a fitness specialist, who can also devise a suitable programme that is tailored towards the ability and experience of the player.

The Training Year

The year can be conveniently split into a number of training phases, where the emphasis of the training regime can be adjusted to suit the needs of the player and her team at each particular point in time:

- The off-season – usually May to June. As the playing season ends, this becomes the time to rest and recover. No football should be played, although other recreational sports can be undertaken.
- Pre-season – usually June to August. This is a period of preparation for the coming season, where the coach would look to develop performance by improving the squad's overall level of fitness.
- Peak-season – usually August to April. This is the playing season and because it is so long, it can be divided into sub-phases, where the emphasis changes according to the demands of the match-play schedule.

Medical Issues

Injury

Football is a contact sport, consequently any player competing at any level is at risk from injury, and injuries

Side-leg kicks.

Groin stretch.

are not limited just to match play, they can occur off the pitch and at training.

With participation levels and playing standards improving year on year, FIFA, as well as national governing bodies, have begun to monitor women's football injuries more closely and they are finding some significant differences in the numbers and types of injuries from those in the men's game:

- 50 per cent of injuries in men's football come from foul play; in women's football, the figure is 30 per cent. It is also significant that of these injuries, 45 per cent occur to the player who made the tackle rather than the player being tackled. In the men's game, only 30 per cent of the players making the tackle end up with an injury.
- Women sustain more head injuries than men, with the contact being head-to-head as opposed to the head-to-elbow injuries sustained in the men's game.
- Women are more at risk from tackles from the side and sliding tackles. Very few injuries occur from tackles from behind.
- Most injuries are to the leg, more specifically the ankle, knee and thigh. There is also a worrying trend of anterior cruciate ligament (ACL) injuries to female players. The ACL is the major stabilizing ligament in the knee and, when it is damaged, the player is likely to need reconstructive surgery. She should plan to be out of the game for an absolute minimum of 6 months and, in some cases, it can signal the end of her career.

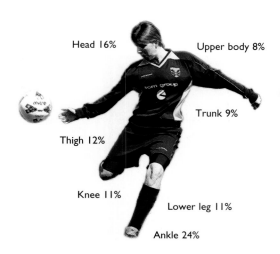

Head 16%

Upper body 8%

Trunk 9%

Thigh 12%

Knee 11%

Lower leg 11%

Ankle 24%

Location of injuries by percentage.

Injury-Prevention Strategies

Some injuries are complete accidents and cannot be predicted, but many others are the result of a predictable set of circumstances. In order to minimize the risks a simple prevention strategy can be easily added to the weekly training programme.

Ankle Injuries

Ankle sprains are the most common joint injury in football and occur when the sole of the foot rolls inwards damaging the ligaments on the outside of the joint. An ankle injury is not always the result of contact and may also occur when a foot is placed, or lands, on an uneven surface. Full recovery from this type of injury can take up to 6 months, but having weakened the ankle once, the player is always likely to injure it again.

Preventative training should focus on improving balance and co-ordination, which helps to develop the flexibility of the joint. There are many simple exercises using just the ground as a base, though it is more effective to incorporate equipment such as ankle discs and wobble boards. The wobble board is undoubtedly the best piece of equipment as it provides an unstable base on which the player has to undertake balance exercises.

ACL Injuries

FIFA have found that 70 per cent of all ACL injuries are non-contact and result from a sudden change of direction, a sudden change of speed or following a jump where the landing was with the knee or hip on full extension. An ACL tear is a serious injury and will mean at least 6 months out of the game, if not longer; in some cases it can also be severe enough to end a playing career. Following damage to the ACL, a player will most likely need reconstructive surgery followed by extensive rehabilitation. With any injury, the temptation is always to rush the process and start playing again too soon. However, in these types of injury there are no shortcuts and inadequate rehabilitation will lead to long-term problems and instability.

Preventative training should focus on stabilizing the knee by strengthening the quadriceps and hamstring muscles, as well as improving balance. Because the quadriceps extend the knee and the hamstrings flex the knee, it is important that both muscle groups are developed together in order to prevent imbalance and therefore create conditions that will lead to instability. Developmental stretching, basic plyometrics and general strengthening activities, which are normally included in a good conditioning programme, are all suitable activities that help to minimize the risks from an ACL tear.

Head Injuries

This group of injuries covers everything from bruises and minor abrasions to more severe fractures and concussion. The injury is sustained following the impact of another hard object to the head, although it is important to make the distinction here between accidental impact and a ball that has been deliberately and correctly headed. It should be noted that when a player is prepared for the impact of the ball and has used good technique, there is very little risk of incurring any sort of head injury.

Concussion has the most potential for causing serious long-term problems, as it is not always easy to diagnose. It results from a temporary loss of brain function following a major or even a minor impact, and it should be noted that a player can be concussed without having noticeably lost consciousness. The effects of concussion cannot always be seen straight away and recovery could be a matter of minutes or months. When it occurs, the safest decision is to keep the player out of the game until she has been properly checked out and cleared by a medical professional.

A player who exhibits any of the signs or symptoms of concussion must immediately cease playing or training. If she has been unconscious, she must go to hospital to be checked out by a medical professional. If there has been no unconsciousness, she should be monitored over the next 24 hours and preferably not left alone during this time.

SIGNS AND SYMPTOMS OF CONCUSSION

Signs (observed)	Symptoms (felt and reported by the player)
Appears dazed	Headache
Staring, vacant expression	Nausea and vomiting
Confused	Dizzy, poor balance
Disorientated	Blurred or double vision
Emotional	Feeling 'out of sorts'
Slurred speech, slow to answer questions	Struggling to concentrate
Lost consciousness	Irritable and emotional
Loss of memory	Loss of memory
Tired and low on energy	Feels tired

Potentially serious complications can develop, even from the most minor head injuries; therefore, if the player suffers from a persistent headache, excessive drowsiness, vomiting, confusion or an extreme change in mood during the next 24 hours, she should also be checked out by the hospital.

Basic Treatment for Minor Injuries

When a player suffers a minor injury, the raised heart-rate and increased circulation will continue to take blood to the muscles where it will be deposited in the injured tissue causing swelling and pain. To slow the bleeding and begin the healing process, there is a simple procedure to follow known by the acronym RICE.

- R is for Rest. The player should stop all activity and rest the injured limb in order to protect it from further damage.
- I is for Ice. An application of ice slows the blood flow and limits the swelling. The ice should be wrapped in a thin piece of fabric and not applied directly to the skin. It should be held against the swelling for 15 minutes with 20 minutes between applications.
- C is for Compression. The injured area should be compressed with a bandage to prevent further swelling and encourage the healing to begin as soon as possible.
- E is for Elevation. Elevating the injured tissue, especially if it can be raised above the heart, also helps to reduce the swelling.

Note: Heat should never be applied to a swelling as this encourages circulation, causing further bleeding and swelling.

To have a maximum effect, RICE treatment should begin as soon as possible after the injury occurred and be continued for about 48 hours, if possible. After this time, if the swelling hasn't begun to subside, the injury should be checked out by a medical professional.

The Female Athlete Triad

For most women footballers their involvement in sport is part of a healthy and balanced lifestyle. However, some are at risk from a syndrome known as the female athlete triad. This is a combination of three interrelated conditions and anyone who works with female players should be familiar with the issues. It should also be noted that a player can be affected by all three conditions or just some of the triad.

Stretching as part of a warm-up routine.

Hydration as part of a training regime.

- Eating disorders. At the root of the triad is the eating disorder, and serious problems will occur when food intake isn't sufficient to cover the body's needs. This could be caused by a deliberate attempt to lose weight by avoiding certain types of food, or it could be the result of a poor diet.
- Amenorrhea. This term relates to the absence of the menstrual period. It is caused by an insufficient calorific intake and is a feature in the lives of many female athletes. However, a prolonged period of amenorrhea can lead to severe health problems, which affect the immune system and reproductive organs.
- Osteoporosis. Low levels of oestrogen, caused by the loss of a period allied to a poor nutritional intake, can cause a loss of bone density leaving the player at risk from stress fractures and more frequent muscle injuries. It is important that the player maintains a calcium-rich diet, and avoids smoking and alcohol as much as possible.

Signs to look out for:

- Weight loss or fluctuation in weight.
- Irregular periods, or none at all.
- Excessive fatigue.

- Stress fracture or frequent muscle injury.
- Over-obsession with body image, diet and weight loss.

Nutrition and Hydration for the Female Athlete

In very simple terms, food provides the fuel that keeps the body running, whilst water provides the lubricant. The nutritional needs will vary from player to player, depending upon the amount of training that they undertake on a weekly or a daily basis. However, the principle remains the same for all players: the diet should support the activity, keeping the player healthy, as well as fuelling her performance.

There is no need for supplements or sophisticated foods, just a common-sense approach towards eating a balanced and well-rounded diet. The benefits of a good diet are plain for all to see:

- Improved recovery between activities.
- Reduced risk from injury.
- Reduced risk from illness.
- More consistency of performance.

Carbohydrates

This food group provides the fuel. It is best to eat naturally-occurring sources, rather than processed food, which can contain an excessively high sugar content. Good sources would be fruit, vegetables and grains, such as brown rice and oatmeal.

Protein

Proteins are required to keep the muscles healthy. This food group also maintains the immune system and aids recovery following exercise. Good sources of protein are fish, eggs, yoghurt, lean red meat, chicken and freshly-made fruit smoothies.

Fat

Fat protects the body's vital organs and helps to insulate it from the cold. More importantly for the athlete, however, the fat stores provide the long-lasting stores of

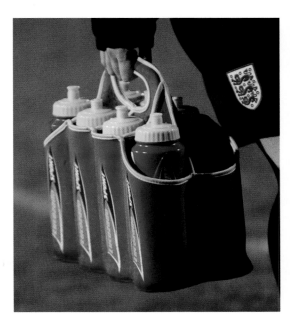

Match hydration.

energy after the carbohydrates have run out. It is best to eat foods containing unsaturated fat whenever possible but the benefits of chocolate, crisps, cakes and biscuits should not be ignored, so long as they are consumed in moderation.

Hydration

If food provides the fuel, then fluid is the lubricant to keep the body healthy during exercise. Dehydration, even mild dehydration, can affect performance and it is important that players drink throughout the day as well as before and after exercise. It should also be stressed that players must drink during every 15–20 minutes of exercise, even in cold weather, in order to replace the fluids lost through physical exertion.

Sports drinks provide taste and a small amount of essential minerals, although water or diluted squash is equally effective in most circumstances. Carbonated drinks should be avoided at all costs.

CHAPTER 11

THE MENTAL GAME

Social and psychological factors are important features affecting cohesion within the team group and should not be overlooked by the coach, as they have a major impact on the quality and consistency of performance.

Every football team is comprised of a diverse group of individuals, all of whom have their own reasons for playing the game, as well as their own very personal set of expectations. Each player is the product of their family and social background, and this has a massive effect on their own personal self-esteem, their confidence and status within the group.

The mental game can be developed and improved by using specific techniques that are aimed at awakening an individual's self-awareness, as well as improving her understanding of the whys and hows of her performance. However, this is often best left to a specialist sports psychologist whose work will complement that of the coach, but who has the added luxury of being able to work one-to-one with each individual, so that her personal needs can be properly addressed.

However, there are some basic strategies that can be consistently re-enforced so that the foundations for cohesion within the group are firmly established.

Vision

To begin with there is a dream where the long-term aims of the team or club are established. These can vary massively from team to team but should be established in order to allow a clear pathway and timescale to be planned. The vision provides the foundations from which all else is built and ensures that everyone who is involved is aware of the aims and is prepared to work together to achieve them.

Typical long-term aims could be:

- Progression through the playing pyramid to a specified higher level.

- Provision of playing opportunities for women from a specific culture or background.
- Player development to feed into a more senior team or organization.

Values

The values are developed once the vision is defined. These essentially help to create the culture of the team by defining the principles of behaviour and providing guidelines for interaction. Values provide cohesion and help to develop a sense of purpose and community. However, they should be applied consistently in order to have meaning. For example, a team that wishes to progress through the playing pyramid would need to think about how they will establish a winning culture, whereas a team that wishes to provide playing opportunities may be more concerned with the social nature of the team environment.

LEFT: Remi Allen showing determination and commitment.

RIGHT: Rachel Yankey proudly shows off the women's FA cup.

The Norwegian women's national team prepare to kick off.

Cause

Vision provides direction and values shape the environment, together both create meaning and provide a cause to which the player can choose to belong. She now has motivation and the team becomes something to commit to, to believe in and to fight for.

Culture

Chapter 3 has already outlined the importance of an open and inclusive player-centred environment. It should be stressed in the context of this chapter that such an environment ensures that the player feels valued and encourages her to actively participate in the ongoing development of the team. In addition, when sessions are challenging, they tend to have multiple outcomes and the player's motivation to belong to the team now becomes her inspiration to perform to the best or her ability for it.

Developing the Individual

For many coaches, performance stems from the mind and there are five factors that should be considered when assessing a player's psychological attributes.

Confidence

This is an optimistic 'can do' mindset that sustains the player through adversity and challenge. Confidence is at the heart of all performance and a confident player will have a strong belief in self, will be able to take responsibility and also make difficult decisions.

For many female players it can be a fragile state of mind, sometimes even being determined by an illogical response to an unintentional comment or action on the part of the coach or a team-mate.

Conditions that help to bolster confidence:

- Consistent environment.
- Positive communication.
- Constant reinforcement through the use of key words and repetition.
- Trust and respect between team members.
- Clear, realistic and achievable goals.

Commitment

Players that are committed refuse to give in, they are able to bounce back from set-backs and will rise to a challenge. Their commitment can be seen both on and off the pitch in the way they play, train and communicate.

Conditions to nurture commitment would include:

- Clear, realistic and achievable long-term aims.
- A strong team identity.
- Feeling valued and respected.
- Short-term, personal goals that can be measured and evaluated.

Concentration

A player who is able to concentrate will be able to remain focused over both the short and the long term. A short-term example of concentration could be during a game where the player's response to distractions in the crowd or an overwhelming fatigue might become a defining feature in the outcome of the game. Over the longer term, examples could include a player focusing on developing a particular part of her game or her fitness levels.

Concentration is a habit that must be practised by providing:

- A mentally and physically challenging environment.
- Training at a match pace.
- Inclusive coaching styles to encourage involvement from the player.

Control

Football is an emotional game full of continual challenges. The successful player will be able to remain stable and exercise self-control, instead of showing an extreme reaction to her emotions. She must learn how to channel her emotions into her performance, rather than allowing them to disrupt it.

Simple strategies to develop control would include:

- Allowing the players to develop and administer a code of behaviour for games and training.
- Providing safe opportunities in small groups to talk and explore emotional reactions to the game.

Communication

Football is a large-team game with performance being dependent upon the interaction between a wide variety of people, all of whom are constantly giving and receiving information from each other. Good communication is fundamental to the team chemistry and crucial if it is to perform in a cohesive fashion. Female players, in particular, must be made to understand that performance is not about playing in a team full of friends, it's about being able to accept each other, tolerate the differences and work together for the long-term benefit of the team.

Conditions to promote good communication would include:

- A consistent and positive environment.
- Inclusive coaching styles that encourage active involvement from each player.
- Respectful behaviour between everyone within the team.
- The coach showing no recognizable favourites.
- Clear and realistic goals over the long and short term.

Larking about after training.

BIBLIOGRAPHY

Bangsbo, J. and Peiterson, B. *Soccer systems and strategies* (Human Kinetics, 2000).
Beswick, B. *Focused for soccer* (Human Kinetics, 2000).
Dorrance, A. *Training soccer champions* (JTC Sports, 1996).
Hamm, M. *Go for the goal* (IT Books, 2000).
Longman, J. *The girls of summer* (IT Books, 2001).
Lopez, S. *Women on the ball* (Scarlet Press, 1997).
Smith, S. *Goalkeeping for soccer* (Coachwise Ltd, 1997).
Williams, J. *A game for rough girls* (Routledge, 2003).

FIFA publications:
The laws of the game (2009/2010).
Health and fitness for the female football player (2007).
Coaching manual (2007).

INDEX

WOMEN'S SOCCER

BNKY